BARRON'S BOOK NOTES

WILLIAM SHAKESPEARE'S

The Tempest

BARRON'S BOOK NOTES

WILLIAM SHAKESPEARE'S

The Tempest

BY

Jeremy Jericho

SERIES COORDINATOR

Murray Bromberg
Principal, Wang High School of Queens
Holliswood, New York

Past President
High School Principals Association of New York City

ACKNOWLEDGMENT

Loreto Todd, Senior Lecturer in English, University of Leeds, England, prepared the chapter on Elizabethan English in this book.

All inquiries should be addressed to:
Barron's Educational Series, Inc.
250 Wireless Boulevard
Hauppauge, New York 11788

Library of Congress Catalog Card No. 85-3973

International Standard Book No. 0-8120-3545-3

Library of Congress Cataloging-in-Publication Data
Jericho, Jeremy.
    William Shakespeare's The tempest.

    (Barron's book notes)
    Bibliography: p. 129
    Summary: A guide to reading ''The Tempest'' with a critical and appreciative mind. Includes background on the author's life and times, sample tests, term paper suggestions, and a reading list.
    1. Shakespeare, William, 1564–1616. Tempest.
    [1. Shakespeare, William, 1564–1616. Tempest.
    2. English literature—History and criticism]
    I. Title. II. Series.
PR2833.J4 1986   822.3'3   85-3973
ISBN 0-8120-3545-3

PRINTED IN THE UNITED STATES OF AMERICA

123   550   98765432

CONTENTS

ADVISORY BOARD

HOW TO USE THIS BOOK

You have to know how to approach literature in order to get the most out of it. This *Barron's Book Notes* volume follows a plan based on methods used by some of the best students to read a work of literature.

Begin with the guide's section on the author's life and times. As you read, try to form a clear picture of the author's personality, circumstances, and motives for writing the work. This background usually will make it easier for you to hear the author's tone of voice, and follow where the author is heading.

Then go over the rest of the introductory material—such sections as those on the plot, characters, setting, themes, and style of the work. Underline, or write down in your notebook, particular things to watch for, such as contrasts between characters and repeated literary devices. At this point, you may want to develop a system of symbols to use in marking your text as you read. (Of course, you should only mark up a book you own, not one that belongs to another person or a school.) Perhaps you will want to use a different letter for each character's name, a different number for each major theme of the book, a different color for each important symbol or literary device. Be prepared to mark up the pages of your book as you read. Put your marks in the margins so you can find them again easily.

Now comes the moment you've been waiting for— the time to start reading the work of literature. You may want to put aside your *Barron's Book Notes* volume until you've read the work all the way through. Or you may want to alternate, reading the *Book Notes* analysis of each section as soon as you have finished reading the corresponding part of the original. Before you move on, reread crucial passages you don't fully understand. (Don't take this guide's analysis for granted—make up your own mind as to what the work means.)

Once you've finished the whole work of literature, you may want to review it right away, so you can firm up your ideas about what it means. You may want to leaf through the book concentrating on passages you marked in reference to one character or one theme. This is also a good time to reread the *Book Notes* introductory material, which pulls together insights on specific topics.

When it comes time to prepare for a test or to write a paper, you'll already have formed ideas about the work. You'll be able to go back through it, refreshing your memory as to the author's exact words and perspective, so that you can support your opinions with evidence drawn straight from the work. Patterns will emerge, and ideas will fall into place; your essay question or term paper will almost write itself. Give yourself a dry run with one of the sample tests in the guide. These tests present both multiple-choice and essay questions. An accompanying section gives answers to the multiple-choice questions as well as suggestions for writing the essays. If you have to select a term paper topic, you may choose one from the list of suggestions in this book. This guide also provides you with a reading list, to help you when you start research for a term paper, and a selection of provocative comments by critics, to spark your thinking before you write.

THE AUTHOR AND HIS TIMES

When Shakespeare wrote *The Tempest*, he was approaching the end of a long, productive, and highly successful career in the theater. He was respected by his fellow playwrights, and was possibly the most popular playwright of his day—though his considerable reputation wasn't nearly as dazzling as it is now. Today, of course, few people would argue that the world has produced a greater writer, in any language, than William Shakespeare. Yet when it comes to his life, we don't have a great deal of information, and guesswork outweighs the facts.

Actually, however, we do know more facts about Shakespeare than about most of the other dramatists of Renaissance England. Unfortunately, those facts—gleaned from some forty documents that name Shakespeare and many more that refer to members of his family—don't reveal much. We're not even sure of the exact date of Shakespeare's birth—the first document that mentions him records his baptism, on April 26, 1564, in Stratford-on-Avon, the quiet village where he was born. We accept April 23 as his birthdate since children were generally baptized three days after their birth. Today Stratford has become a literary shrine to which tourists from all over the world travel to see performances by the Royal Shakespeare Company. Four centuries after his birth, Shakespeare's plays are still performed more than any other playwright's, living or dead.

Shakespeare's father was comfortably well-off; he had married the daughter of a wealthy land-owner, and he owned a business that dealt in leather goods (such as gloves) and farm commodities. John Shakespeare also dabbled in local affairs. By 1568 he had risen to the post of high bailiff, the equivalent of mayor; but for some reason he dropped out of politics, and suffered some financial setbacks.

We know nothing of Shakespeare's schooling, but it's probable that as the son of a public official he attended the town's grammar school, where he would have received a fine education in Latin. He would draw on his knowledge of Latin rhetoric, logic, and literature in his later playwriting. (Prospero's farewell to his art, for example, in Act V of *The Tempest*, owes something to the *Metamorphoses* of the Roman poet Ovid.) In 1582 Shakespeare married Anne Hathaway, who was eight years his senior. She was pregnant at the time of the marriage, since Susanna Shakespeare was born six months later. It was considered permissible, in Shakespeare's England, for engaged couples to sleep together, so there's no reason to assume it was a forced wedding. In 1585 the couple had twins, Hamnet and Judith. Hamnet, Shakespeare's only son, died two years later.

Some time after the birth of the twins, Shakespeare left Stratford for London. There's a tradition that he was forced to leave Stratford because he was caught poaching (illegally hunting) deer on a local aristocrat's land, but there's no firm evidence to verify this. According to another tradition, he became a country schoolteacher; some people have suggested that he worked as a traveling actor. It was time when country towns like

Stratford were declining in prosperity. London was the main center of opportunity for ambitious young men and women, so it's not surprising that Shakespeare went there to seek his fortune.

Nobody knows when or how Shakespeare became involved in the theater, but he made a name for himself in a relatively brief time. By 1592, when he was just twenty-eight, he was attacked by a rival playwright, Robert Greene. Greene wrote a pamphlet in which he sneered at Shakespeare as an "upstart crow," a mere actor who, with no university education, had the nerve to think he could write plays. (Attacks on Shakespeare's education would continue to plague him. Even several years after his death, his great contemporary Ben Jonson could accuse him, in a poem that's otherwise complimentary, of having "small Latin, and less Greek." Study of the plays, however, proves that this wasn't altogether just.) Shakespeare must have been quite popular by the time of Greene's attack, because it drew complaints, and Greene's editor apologized to Shakespeare in Greene's next pamphlet.

During his career as a playwright, Shakespeare continued to act as well, though the profession was considered slightly beneath anything a real gentleman might undertake. He was listed in a document in 1598 as a "principal comedian," and in 1603 as a "principal tragedian." In 1594 he became one of the founders of a company called the Chamberlain's Men, which he remained with for the rest of his career. When James I took the throne after the death of Queen Elizabeth in 1603, the company became the King's Men. The name change indicated royal support: from then on, they enjoyed the official status of servants of the King.

All this meant profits for Shakespeare. He earned

one tenth of the take at the Globe Theatre, where the Chamberlain's Men performed. (He was the only London dramatist who held a share in a theater.) He bought real estate in Stratford, where he had become a famous native son. In 1597 he purchased a fine house in the town—the house to which he retired not long after he wrote *The Tempest*.

From about 1592 to about 1612 (the dates of most of the plays are conjectures), Shakespeare produced some thirty-seven plays that are as rich and varied as anything in the body of world literature. They're remarkable for the beauty of their verse and for the intensity and nuance with which Shakespeare delves into the psychology of his characters. In addition, their wide range is amazing. The First Folio of Shakespeare's collected works, published in 1623, seven years after his death, divided them into comedies, histories, and tragedies; they range in tone and subject matter from the highjinks of *A Midsummer Night's Dream* to the gentle melancholy of *As You Like It* to the political philosophizing of *Henry IV* to the bitter ironies of *Hamlet* to the almost unbearable agonies of *King Lear*. The plays are stunningly profound and complex. But toward the end of his career, Shakespeare began writing a different kind of drama— much lighter, much simpler, much less psychological; you could almost call these plays fairy tales. (Most critics refer to them as "romances".) But their simplicity is a kind of purity—not the simplicity of shallowness, or of a playwright who can't handle anything more difficult, but a simplicity that goes beyond complexity. First Shakespeare wrote *Pericles*, then *Cymbeline*, then *The Winter's Tale*; finally, with *The Tempest*, he perfected this interesting form. After he wrote *The Tempest*, he left London and apparently retired from the theater. The last plays, *Henry VIII* and possibly *The Two Noble Kinsmen*, were probably collaborations with other playwrights. He died in Stratford in 1616.

* * *

For most of his working life, Shakespeare was associated with the Globe Theatre. It was an open-air theater located across the Thames from London proper, so that it was out of the city's jurisdiction. It was round or octagonal; inside, the stage jutted halfway out into the yard. There was a second story above the stage that could be used for a balcony scene, as in *Romeo and Juliet*, or for the battlements in *Hamlet*; above that, a third story held the musicians' gallery. On the very top, a flag waving from a turret announced the day's performance.

The cheapest tickets, at one penny (a day's wage for an apprentice), admitted you to the yard, where you stood with the other "groundlings" to watch the play. Another penny would buy you a seat in the upper galleries, and a third would get you a cushioned seat in the lower gallery—the best seats in the house. Sets were simple, but costumes were ornate. The audience was diverse—theater held a position in Shakespeare's England similar to the position movies hold today. People of all social classes went to the theater, so Shakespeare had to include something in his plays for everyone. There had to be erudition to appeal to the scholars; there were clowns who made awful puns, as Trinculo does in *The Tempest*, for the spectators in the yard. And of course Shakespeare had to be careful that nothing he wrote would offend the King, for whom

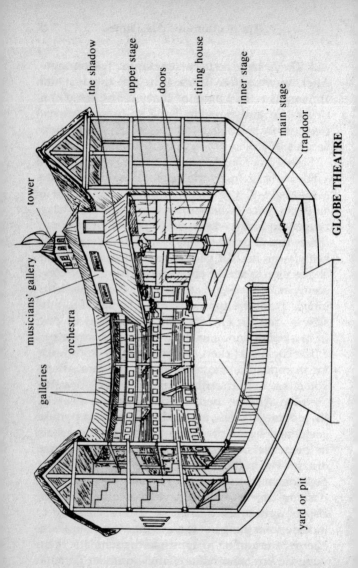

the shadow

upper stage

doors

tiring house

inner stage

main stage

trapdoor

tower

musicians' gallery

orchestra

galleries

yard or pit

GLOBE THEATRE

the King's Men performed at court. For example, Shakespeare had to be sensitive in his presentation of Prospero as a magician. James I considered himself an authority on magic, and if Shakespeare had seemed to endorse black magic he could have landed in jail.

Since the Globe was an open-air theater, it couldn't be used during cold weather. During the winter, the King's Men performed at court or in one of London's indoor theaters. In 1608, Shakespeare and six partners took over the Blackfriars Theatre, which was much more like the theaters we're used to: a large indoor room, artificially lit. Admission to the indoor theaters was more expensive, and the stage machinery was more sophisticated. *The Tempest* may well have been acted at the Globe—the King's Men used both theaters after 1608—but it was almost certainly performed at Blackfriars, and the kind of spectacle in the play suggests that it was conceived with the sophisticated indoor theater in mind. The extensive music in the play also seems more appropriate to an indoor theater. Music was an important and popular element of Globe performances, appealing as it did to every class of spectator; however, in an indoor theater you could achieve more subtle musical effects because the acoustics were so much better. That's probably one reason there's so much music, especially instrumental music, in *The Tempest*.

We know the play was acted at court, because there's a record of a performance attended by the King at Whitehall Palace on November 1, 1611. This was an early performance, perhaps even the first. The play is fairly easy to date. It can't have been written later than that 1611 performance, and it can't have been written before 1610, because passages in it rely on the "Bermuda pamphlets" (see the section on Sources), which were published that year.

THE PLAY

The Plot

A ship at sea is the victim of a fierce tempest (storm). The terrified passengers include Alonso, the King of Naples; his son Ferdinand; his brother Sebastian; his kind old councilor Gonzalo; and Antonio, the false Duke of Milan. The men don't know it, but the storm has brought them to the island of the magician Prospero (who conjured up the tempest) and his daughter Miranda.

Prospero is the real Duke of Milan. Twelve years earlier, he had been overthrown by his younger brother Antonio. With the help of Alonso and Sebastian, Antonio drove Prospero and Prospero's daughter Miranda out of Milan and had them cast out to sea. But divine providence brought them to the island. Prospero has two servants: the airy spirit Ariel, through whom he commands other, lesser spirits; and Caliban, a monster he found on the island and treated kindly until Caliban tried to rape Miranda. Now Prospero rules him sternly.

Prospero has a plan to deal with his old enemies. He's separated Alonso's son, Prince Ferdinand, from the others. When Ferdinand and Miranda meet, they quickly fall in love. But Prospero wants to make sure that Ferdinand fully deserves his daughter, so he tests him with the heavy task of piling a thousand logs before sunset.

King Alonso, meanwhile, is grief-stricken, because he thinks Prince Ferdinand has drowned. His councilor Gonzalo tries to comfort him; Gonzalo believes deeply in divine providence, though Antonio and Sebastian jeer at his optimism. These two plot to kill Alonso and Gonzalo as they sleep, so Sebastian can usurp his brother's crown just as Antonio stole Prospero's. But Ariel wakes the king and his councilor before the two villains can drive their swords into them.

Two other survivors of the tempest are Stephano, a drunken butler who's managed to salvage a keg of wine, and Trinculo, a jester. They encounter Caliban, and soon all three are roaring drunk. Caliban takes these fools for gods who will free him from his slavery to Prospero; together they scheme to kill the magician. But Trinculo and Caliban squabble, especially after Ariel starts doing mischief. The invisible spirit keeps calling Caliban a liar; Stephano thinks the insult comes from Trinculo, and eventually he pummels the innocent jester. Before they can set their scheme against Prospero in motion, Ariel leads them off with enchanted music, then goes to report the scheme to his master.

The King's party, discouraged in its search for Ferdinand, stops to rest. Ariel and the other spirits prepare a banquet for the group, but then turn into harpies and snatch it away. As the men look on astonished and terrified, Ariel tells the guilty ones (Alonso, Sebastian, and Antonio) that they're being punished for their crime against Prospero. The spirit's voice sends them into a maddened frenzy.

Ferdinand, meanwhile, has passed his test. After Prospero lectures the young man to remain chaste until the marriage, the spirits entertain the lovers with a masque, in which the goddesses Iris, Ceres, and Juno wish the couple a prosperous and happy life. The masque ends abruptly when Prospero remembers Caliban's plot on his life and starts up in anger. He and Ariel lure the plotters with expensive clothing. Stephano and Trinculo are so carried away by the loot that they forget about their scheme. Suddenly Prospero and Ariel unleash the spirits, who attack the conspirators fiercely with pinches and cramps.

Prompted, perhaps, by Ariel, Prospero has decided to forgive his old enemies. He brings Alonso, Sebastian, and Antonio before him, along with Gonzalo and the rest of the King's party. After removing the spell that had maddened them, he reveals his identity. Alonso quickly asks his pardon, though Antonio and Sebastian never really repent. To Alonso's delight, Ferdinand turns out to be not only alive but betrothed to the lovely Miranda as well. Ariel leads in the captain of the ship and the boatswain, who declares that the ship they'd thought was ruined is—incredibly—in perfect condition (more of Ariel's magic). When Ariel brings in Caliban, Stephano, and Trinculo, they're in sorry shape from the punishing spirits. Prospero forgives Caliban, too. He's decided to give up his magic and return with the others as the rightful Duke of Milan. After commanding Ariel to speed their trip, Prospero promises the airy spirit the freedom he's wanted for so long.

The Characters

Prospero

Prospero stands at the very center of *The Tempest*. He has more lines than any other character. He prompts most of the action, and he has the last word. He's contradictory, a difficult character to evaluate.

He was once the Duke of Milan, but a love of study led him to leave governing to his brother Antonio; the treacherous Antonio then drove him out of Milan. Later, on his island, he lovingly educated the monster Caliban and gave him freedom. Caliban returned that kindness by trying to rape Prospero's daughter, Miranda. Prospero makes essentially the same mistake with both Antonio and Caliban: he fails to keep them in their proper place, and he fails to exercise his responsibilities. It may be an error on the side of kindness, but it's an error all the same, and he and others suffer because of it. It makes him a less than perfect ruler.

If Prospero has a lesson to learn, however, he's learned it by the time the play opens. The Prospero you see exemplifies wisdom, justice, and superhuman good judgment. This near-faultlessness has led some readers to regard Prospero as a representation, in human terms, of God. Prospero stands in relation to the other characters as God does to humanity: judging, punishing, and forgiving. (Thanks to Ariel, he's all-knowing too.) But he's an Old Testament God, prone to vengeful fury when he's crossed, and quite willing to look on calmly while those in his power are punished. You could argue that the sufferings of Caliban, Stephano, and Trinculo are comic; however, there's something cruel in the way Prospero toys with his old enemy Alonso, letting him think until the last minute that his beloved son Ferdinand is dead. (Bringing Ferdinand back from the dead, so to speak, is Godlike too.) But if Prospero feels anger, he also overcomes it. Ultimately he's a benevolent figure. Why do you think some readers of this play regard him as even more forgiving than a Christian God?

An equally popular view is that Prospero is a stand-in for Shakespeare. Prospero is deeply interested in marrying off his daughter; Shakespeare was the father of two daughters, only one of whom had married when *The Tempest* was written. Prospero's time of life is roughly equivalent to Shakespeare's: he's aging and starting to think about death. Supporters of this theory point to the speech (Act V, Scene I, lines 33–57) generally known as Prospero's farewell to his art, in which he declares that he'll abandon magic when he leaves the island. Since *The Tempest* is probably the last play that Shakespeare wrote, or wrote alone, and since not long after he wrote it he left London for a quiet retirement in Stratford-on-Avon, many readers have interpreted Prospero's speech as Shakespeare's farewell to his own art. These readers say that Prospero's magic stands for Shakespeare's poetry, and that Prospero's breaking of his wand symbolizes Shakespeare laying down his pen. But there's an equally adamant group of readers who argue that it's unnecessary to look outside *The Tempest* for its meaning, when there's so much meaning before you on the page.

Prospero is a disturbing, even contradictory mixture of blanket forgiveness and almost wanton cruelty—although many would argue that his enemies deserved harsh treatment. Even if you accept his vengeful pleasure in tormenting Alonso, Sebastian, and Antonio, you still have to ask: Why does he let kind old Gonzalo suffer too? Why does he nearly break Miranda's heart by letting her think he hates Ferdinand? It may be that these moral and psychological issues are exactly the kinds of questions you shouldn't be asking about the play. You face a fundamental problem in trying to analyze Prospero (and most of the other characters in *The Tempest*), and this problem stems from the type of work *The Tempest* is. Late in his career, Shakespeare wrote four "romances"—*Pericles*, *Cymbeline*, *The Winter's Tale*, and *The Tempest*—that are much simpler in technique than his earlier plays, almost like fairy tales. They strive not for psychological depth but for lightness, simplicity, and grace. If Prospero isn't as complex a man as, say, Hamlet, it's not because Shakespeare failed to develop his character adequately, but because he was striving toward a very different goal.

There is one psychological trait, however, that Shakespeare clearly means you to observe, and even condemn, in Prospero, because he wants to make a moral point about it. This trait is anger. Late in the fourth act, Prospero interrupts the spirits' pleasant masque when he's suddenly overcome with rage at the thought of Caliban's plot against him. Then, early in Act V, he admits to Ariel that he can only forgive his enemies by letting his "nobler reason" overcome his all-too-evident "fury." This fury, more than any other quality, makes Prospero a flesh-and-blood human being instead of a stick-figure wise man. But it doesn't always make him a likable character. You might think of the last time you were furious about something in order to achieve a better understanding of Prospero's behavior. Did you handle yourself better than he did?

Ariel

The "airy spirit" can assume different shapes (flame, nymph, or harpy), and it's through him that Prospero commands the lesser spirits. Ariel is all lightness, quickness, and grace. But his foremost characteristic is intelligence; he's practically made of intelligence, and he even moves with the speed of thought. ("Come with a thought," Prospero tells him in Act IV, Scene I.) It's part of his nature—as, perhaps, it's characteristic of thought—to be free. Thus, he serves Prospero loyally but not willingly, in return for Prospero's aid in freeing him from the cloven pine tree, where the witch Sycorax had imprisoned him.

Ariel declares in Act V, Scene I, that he doesn't have human emotions. But his mischievous streak— which he displays in the tricks he plays on Caliban, Stephano, and Trinculo—suggests that he has a sense of humor. More importantly, he has a strong moral sense. You can deduce this from his harsh speech to the "three men of sin" (Act III, Scene III), in which he stresses the themes of justice and repentance. Of course, Prospero could have prompted those lines. But you also know, from Prospero's reminiscences in Act I, Scene II, the reason Sycorax imprisoned Ariel in the cloven pine: the good spirit was "too delicate" to carry out her "abhorred commands."

Readers looking for concealed autobiography in *The Tempest* have sometimes argued that Ariel represents a specific aspect of Shakespeare, usually his poetic genius. Ariel certainly is "creative"; he constructs the situations that Prospero has dreamed up for various characters. In addition, he's the most musical of the characters in a play filled with music—he's constantly singing, playing, or calling forth enchanted music, a fact that adds not only to his charm but to his aura of magic too, especially since so many of his songs are both vague and lovely. If Ariel's personality is hard to pin down, it's because he's so light, so misty. He's meant to be mysterious, because he's a magic being.

Caliban

The monster offspring of a witch and a devil, Caliban is a would-be rapist, thief, and killer. Yet it's almost impossible not to like him. Maybe this is because it's easy to see one side of yourself in him: who wouldn't rather lie around in the sun than haul firewood and clean the house? One view of Caliban is that he's too innocent, too childlike to be a full-fledged villain. Like an animal, he simply snatches at what he wants without thinking about right or wrong. He's generally unteachable. Prospero's problems with Caliban, in this view, are really his own fault for failing to recognize the monster for what he is, and giving him an education that only makes him dissatisfied with his low place in the social order.

An opposing view, which Prospero seems to share, regards the "born devil" as a deeply evil being. It's clear that Caliban doesn't repent his attempt to rape Miranda; he only regrets that it was stopped. ("Would't had been done!" he cries in Act I, Scene II.) His lack of any moral sense makes him the opposite of Ariel. In fact, he's almost a negative or anti-Ariel: slow-moving, earthbound, stupid, and lazy. He wants freedom not because it's in his nature but because he hates work. If Ariel's nature embodies freedom, Caliban is by nature a slave. He needs authority because he can't control himself. Those who look for autobiography in *The Tempest* regard him as the dark side of Shakespeare's personality: greed and appetite. The fact that Prospero keeps him chained in a rocky den may signify the poet's self-discipline, the way he keeps his desires under control.

Caliban is also contrasted with Miranda. Prospero carefully nurtures his daughter; her education turns her into a fine, moral young woman. But Caliban is a beast "on whose nature/Nurture can never stick" (Act IV, Scene I); education rolls right off him when it doesn't do outright harm.

Finally, Caliban forms a strong contrast to the real villains of the play, Antonio and Sebastian. The monster strays into crime because he doesn't know better. Antonio and Sebastian, however, do know better; they're noblemen, and their only excuse for their behavior is greed and sinfulness. Perhaps this explains why in the last act Shakespeare suggests that the supposedly unteachable Caliban has learned a lesson: "I'll be wise hereafter/And seek for grace."

As you read you'll note that Caliban is given some of the loveliest poetry in the play. Certainly this is a part of what makes him so likable: any beast who responds to music with Caliban's sensitivity (see the speech in Act III, Scene II) can't be all brute. His poetry also reminds you that, like Ariel, he's a magical being. His coarse cohorts, Stephano and Trinculo, speak prose; Caliban's verse is part of the enchantment of Prospero's island.

Alonso

Alonso, King of Naples, was one of the men who plotted against Prospero; thus, he deserves his punishment on the island. But he isn't a villain on the order of Antonio and Sebastian. Besides, his part in the plot seems to have been mainly political. The deal brought him the annual tribute that Milan paid Naples, and you can at least understand the motivations of a leader who seeks wealth for his realm. But the main reasons that Alonso comes off far better than Antonio and Sebastian are that he's grieving deeply for Ferdinand—you can't help feeling sorry for a bereaved father; and, when confronted with his crime he feels guilty, repents, and asks for pardon.

Alonso is a pessimist, constantly looking on the dark side of things. After the tempest he's certain, although he has no real evidence, that Ferdinand is dead; he refuses to be consoled by the voices of reason. And when at last Prospero reveals to him the living Ferdinand, his first reaction is worry: What if it's an illusion? In the context of a play whose major emphasis is on divine providence, this pessimism is seen by some as a major character flaw. Alonso (as Prospero rebukes him in Act V) lacks patience, and patience is a sign of faith in the God who watches benevolently over human events.

Overall, though, many regard Alonso as a good man if not a great one. His love for his son speaks in his favor, as does his quick acceptance of Miranda as Ferdinand's betrothed. Like everyone else, he's capable of wrongs; however, he's also capable of recognizing them, regretting them, and atoning for them.

Gonzalo

Gonzalo is the voice of patience in *The Tempest*. He probably comes closer than any other character of the older generation to representing Shakespeare's idea of a good Christian, because he's not flawed with Alonso's pessimism or Prospero's anger. Gonzalo always trusts Providence. Even during the tempest he's calm enough to joke about the boatswain's gallows-bound looks, and to find a sign of hope in them. It's Gonzalo who appreciates the miracle of their safety on Prospero's island, Gonzalo who unwaveringly insists that Ferdinand is still alive.

Above all, Gonzalo is loyal. When Antonio and Sebastian plot to murder the King, they know they have to kill Gonzalo too; he would never accept Sebastian as King. Later, when Alonso is maddened by guilt, Gonzalo stands beside him weeping, the most grief-stricken of the mourners.

His kindness extends even further. He oversaw the actual casting-out-to-sea of Prospero and Miranda, and Prospero, rather than feeling bitter toward him, remembers his "charity" with fondness twelve years later. Gonzalo provided the clothing, food, and fresh water that kept them alive, and the beloved books that have allowed Prospero to master the spirits.

But your picture of Gonzalo might not be as sentimental as all this suggests. Shakespeare had a knack for satirizing gabby old men (Polonius in *Hamlet* is a prime example), and he appears to have sketched Gonzalo with a hint of a smile. The old man doesn't deserve the rude jeers of Antonio and Sebastian in Act II, Scene I, but his manner is befuddled and talkative enough to give some point to their jokes. His speech about how he would rule the island (Act II, Scene I) is far more starry-eyed than practical, though it's true that he's chattering mainly to entertain King Alonso and distract him from his grief. In addition, he gets carried away during his great Act V speech on divine providence, ending with the assertion that everybody has attained self-knowledge, which is a long way from the truth. These little imperfections make Gonzalo seem more human than he otherwise might.

Antonio

Antonio is the obvious villain of *The Tempest*. He betrayed his brother Prospero by stealing his dukedom and driving him out of Milan. Once on the island, he plots with Sebastian to kill Alonso and steal his kingdom. He's rude to the boatswain (Act I, Scene I) and to kind old Gonzalo (Act II, Scene I). Despite all the talk about the importance of repentance, he never says he's sorry for anything he's done. In fact, during the reconciliations of Act V he remains silent except for one sarcastic jab at Caliban.

Antonio is a character of little psychological complexity; he's simply evil. The term "motiveless malignancy," which the English poet Samuel Taylor Coleridge devised to describe Iago, the villain of *Othello*, applies equally well to Antonio. If you regard the play from a Christian viewpoint in which Prospero stands for God, Alonso represents the sinner who repents, and Antonio and Sebastian represent unrepentant sinners. The shortcoming with this interpretation is that instead of being damned they're forgiven along with everybody else (though it's probable, considering Prospero's threat of blackmail, that he's planning to keep them on a very short leash).

Without Antonio and Sebastian, *The Tempest* really would seem as light as a fairy tale—especially because Caliban, despite all his wickedness, strikes audiences as such a funny, likable creature. Antonio and Sebastian are sour notes—figures of real, human evil. By letting them off unrepentant, Shakespeare brings the world of *The Tempest* much closer to our own imperfect world. Evil exists, he might be saying, and sometimes it goes unpunished; we can't say why.

Sebastian

Alonso's treacherous brother Sebastian is to some extent a carbon copy of Antonio—not quite as evil, perhaps, since he merely follows Antonio's lead in the scheme to kill Alonso. Though Sebastian, like Antonio, is unrepentant at the end, he's not as sourly silent. His last line, accusing Stephano and Trinculo of theft, is hypocritical enough to be funny.

Ferdinand

If Antonio and Sebastian are thoroughly evil, then Ferdinand and Miranda are completely good. Certainly they're no more complex psychologically—they resemble the brave, handsome prince and the beautiful, sweet princess of a fairy tale.

Ferdinand is the son of Alonso and thus heir to the throne of Naples. He's a dutiful son, grieving for his father when he thinks he's drowned, and begging his pardon for becoming betrothed without his permission when he learns Alonso is alive after all. He's courageous enough to draw a sword against Prospero when the magician threatens him, and patient enough to perform the burdensome task of piling a thousand logs when he knows Miranda is the prize.

Ferdinand's chastity forms a sharp contrast to Caliban's uncontrolled desire. (This subject is the substance of his conversation with Prospero near the beginning of Act IV.) But he's not prissy. The young prince is red-blooded enough for Prospero to have to chastise him (Act IV, Scene I) about embracing Miranda a little too warmly.

Through their children Ferdinand and Miranda, Alonso and Prospero find a way to heal their old enmity. It's easier for them to be reconciled once their son and daughter are betrothed.

Miranda

Miranda's only experience of people—at least since the age of three, when she was cast out to sea with Prospero—has been her father. Thus, she's a bit naive. When she first sees Ferdinand (Act I, Scene II), she thinks he's a spirit; when she sees the royal party (Act V, Scene I), she's so overcome by their splendor that she's convinced they're "goodly creatures," even though two of those creatures are Antonio and Sebastian. (But since Caliban attempted to rape her, she's learned to hate him; she clearly has had some experience of evil.)

Miranda's innocence is her great charm. She's had the best of both worlds: a splendid and civilized education without the corrupting influence of civilization. Because she doesn't know how to be coy, she's straightforward about her feelings for Ferdinand; this lack of cunning is part of what wins his heart. Overcome by Ferdinand's handsomeness, she falls in love with him at once. But the way their love is depicted is so far from realistic that you can't condemn her for overhasty judgment: love at first sight is a convention of the literary form knows as a romance.

Stephano

Stephano is a coarse, drunken brute. He bullies Caliban and Trinculo mercilessly, and he has no qualms about joining a plot to kill Prospero, steal his island, and rape his daughter. But Stephano's wickedness shouldn't be taken too seriously. Like Caliban, he can be excused for having a low nature. He's principally a comic creation whose job is to give the audience some relief from the more serious main plot. Stephano is the kind of character whose slapstick distress makes you laugh. For example, when the goblins attack him and his cohorts at the end of Act IV, it's funny, not awful.

Trinculo

Trinculo probably says less of real intelligence than any of Shakespeare's other jesters, though he does have a jester's ear for a good pun. He always seems to be afraid of something: the weather, Caliban, or Ariel's music. Stephano bullies him, but he follows Stephano's lead in a way that parodies Sebastian's relationship with Antonio.

Boatswain

The boatswain, the officer in charge of the ship's deck crew, is a gruff sailor who's too competent to be intimidated by the interference of Antonio and Sebastian during the tempest. Gonzalo's comments suggest that his appearance is thoroughly disreputable ("perfect gallows"), but the old man's jokes about his blasphemy aren't supported by anything in the text. His oaths may have been spoken onstage but left out of the published version.

Iris, Ceres, Juno

Prospero's spirits imitate these three goddesses of Greek and Roman mythology during the masque, in Act IV, for Ferdinand and Miranda. Iris is the goddess of the rainbow and the messenger of the gods. Ceres oversees the harvest and fertility in general, so her blessing would be important to a couple who want children. Juno, queen of the gods, is the protector of marriage.

Other Elements

SETTING

All the action of *The Tempest* takes place on (or, in the first scene, very close to) the remote island where Prospero and Miranda have spent the last twelve years. The island must be somewhere in the Mediterranean Sea, because Prospero and Miranda were cast out to sea from Italy, and because Alonso's fleet is on its way home to Naples, in Italy, from Tunis, in northern Africa, when the storm strikes. But the island has more in common with the Bermuda Islands in the Atlantic Ocean than with any islands in the Mediterranean. This is because one of Shakespeare's sources was a series of pamphlets that had been written about a recent shipwreck in the Bermudas. (For more information, see the Note about "the still-vexed Bermoothes" in Act I, Scene II.)

Popular superstition held that the Bermudas were aswarm with fairies and demons, just as Prospero's island is. Everything about the island whispers magic, especially the ever-present music that Caliban describes in his beautiful speech, "Be not afeard; the isle is full of noises" (Act III, Scene II).

By setting the play on an island and limiting his cast to a few characters, Shakespeare lets his themes stand out in sharper relief. A court setting would be far more complex; Prospero would have to worry about the influence of current events, and as head of government he'd have to curb his vengeance and act in a way that appeared more responsible. The shipwrecked characters feel lost and forlorn on the island and thus behave with a straightforwardness that would be more guarded if they were in their normal setting.

Once on the island, some of the characters re-create the society from which they came. Gonzalo, for example, is mainly interested in preserving the social order by guarding the well-being of King Alonso. Antonio, ever the schemer, sees in the shipwreck a means for upsetting the social order and seizing more power. Stephano and Trinculo, on the other hand, behave so freely and amorally because they think they're outside the limits of society and have no punishment to fear.

THEMES

1. PROVIDENCE AND PATIENCE

Prospero tells Miranda (Act I, Scene II) that they reached the island "By providence divine"—that is, through the guidance and benevolence of God. Though there are few direct references to God in

The Tempest, this highly Christian theme permeates the play. Ferdinand phrases it briefly in Act V: "Though the seas threaten, they are merciful." *The Tempest* is a play about a storm that turns into a blessing. There are times in all our lives when things may look bleak, even desperate; but a good Christian trusts in the wisdom and mercy of God to bring things to a happy end.

If Prospero represents the workings of providence (he raises the storm and offers the blessing), Gonzalo is the good Christian, the man of faith. (His speech in Act V, Scene I, is the great summation of the providence theme.) Another name for this faith is patience: Gonzalo patiently endures doubt and hardship because his faith sustains him. His firm belief in a just God convinces him that no matter how bad things look, they'll turn out for the best. Alonso, in contrast, is the impatient man, rebuffing Gonzalo's attempts to console him. Because he lacks faith in providence, he insists that Ferdinand is dead and that searching for him is useless. He refuses to believe a just power oversees events, and this doubt signifies a lack of trust in God.

2. FORGIVENESS AND REPENTANCE

The Tempest is clearly a play about reconciliation. What isn't clear is whether Prospero intends from the beginning to forgive his old enemies or whether his mercy is a last-minute decision. The fact that he plans from the first to marry Ferdinand to Miranda would suggest that he had planned a reconciliation with Ferdinand's father, Alonso, all along. On the other hand, however, you can point to the anger that grips Prospero until the end; if he were planning to forgive from the beginning, wouldn't he already have overcome his anger? Those who think he decides only late in the play to forgive, focus especially on Ariel's description, early in Act V, of Alonso and his party in distress, which may be the turning point in prompting Prospero to pity and mercy.

But Prospero's words here lead to a further confusion. "They being penitent," he tells Ariel, is all he wanted—which is essentially what Ariel told the "three men of sin" in his harsh speech near the end of Act III, Scene III. Alonso asks for Prospero's pardon and expresses remorse for his crimes to Miranda as well. Antonio and Sebastian, however, give no hint that they're penitent, when even the bestial Caliban is declaring he'll "be wise hereafter/And seek for grace."

Then why does Prospero forgive these unremorseful villains? That's one of the mysteries of the play. (Even God forgives only sinners who repent.) It may be that Shakespeare considers humanity so depraved that if you only forgave those who deserved it, then nobody would ever be forgiven. Or he may think that the forgiveness itself is what's important, regardless of whether the forgiven party deserves it; as Prospero says, "The rarer action is/In virtue than in vengeance" (Act V, Scene I). But if that's the case, where does justice fit in—isn't it also right to punish criminals, especially unrepentant ones? This is a question to which Shakespeare doesn't provide the answer. What advice might you give to Prospero regarding Antonio and Sebastian?

3. KNOWLEDGE AND ORDER

Shakespeare uses education to contrast Miranda, who has a "high" nature, with "low"-natured Caliban. Miranda's education nurtures her into a fine, moral, and chaste young woman. But Caliban, as Prospero complains in Act IV, Scene I, is a creature "on whose nature/Nurture can never stick"; his education only makes him dissatisfied with his low status. As Caliban says, his main profit from learning language is knowing how to curse.

Prospero made the same mistake with Caliban as he had made with Antonio: he failed to keep them in their proper places, and his leniency gave both of them a taste for a station higher than their own. Shakespeare's audience had a highly developed sense of order—the King ruled by divine right, aristocrats were people with high natures, and the poor drudged at their low station because God intended it that way. Trying to rise above your station was doing exactly what got Satan expelled from heaven.

Knowledge, though precious, can be dangerous if it interferes with order. Adam and Eve ate from the tree of knowledge because they wanted to be "as gods." Prospero, too, lost his dukedom because he neglected governing for studying. Prospero's book may be the source of his power on the island, but he must learn the proper place of knowledge on the scale of values if he is to be a truly wise ruler.

4.   BEAUTY AND VIRTUE

Much is said about beauty in *The Tempest*. Miranda in particular is taken with the way people look. She falls in love at her first sight of Ferdinand's "brave form", and later, when she beholds Alonso and his nobles, she cries,

O, wonder!
How many goodly creatures are there here!

How beauteous mankind is! O brave new world
That has such people in't!
(Act V, Scene I, lines 181–184)

Miranda associates beauty with "goodliness" not only because of Ferdinand, but also because her main image of evil has been Caliban—who, as Prospero informs you in Act IV, Scene I, grows uglier as his mind cankers. Caliban's mother, the "foul witch Sycorax," was equally deformed, "grown into a hoop" with "age and envy" (Act I, Scene II).

Shakespeare's audience believed in a connection between physical and moral beauty; the body, they thought, was a reflection of the soul. (According to Genesis, after all, God created humanity in his own image.) But they weren't quite as naive as Miranda, and neither was Shakespeare: the "goodly creatures" she extols include Antonio and Sebastian, who may look noble but aren't. The theme of beauty-equals-virtue works on a simple, fairy-tale plane in the Miranda-Ferdinand scenes, but before the play is over Shakespeare reminds you that reality isn't as neat.

5. CHASTITY AND APPETITE

A contrast in *The Tempest* is made between Ferdinand, who praises chastity, and Caliban, a creature of uncontrolled desire. (See especially the beginning of Act IV, where Prospero lectures Ferdinand on the subject.) Prospero must learn to control his own appetites, especially for knowledge, and to control his anger.

Though Caliban is the prime example of appetite run amuck, Shakespeare also offers Stephano (a drunkard) and Trinculo—who plan murder, rape, and robbery—as well as Antonio and Sebastian, as horrible examples of what uncontrolled appetites can do to people.

6. OTHER THEMES

The above listing of themes is only a beginning; it doesn't exhaust the thematic richness of *The Tempest*. The list of themes goes on and on. An important one is the *contrast between nature and society*. Nature's representative is Caliban; when you compare him to the wise, just, and *civilized* Prospero you can appreciate the sharp differences. However, society has also produced Antonio and Sebastian, and Caliban compares favorably with these villains. A civilized man may be superior to an uncivilized beast, but the natural beast is better than the depraved products of society.

Another important theme might be called *purification through suffering*. Prospero, in his long exile, has more than atoned for whatever mistakes he might have made when he ruled Milan. Ferdinand must suffer through Prospero's tests before he can win Miranda's hand. Most significantly, Alonso must undergo the suffering that Prospero has designed for him before Prospero can find it in his heart to forgive him. Prospero has created a Purgatory for Alonso and his companions on the island; only after they're purged is he ready to show them his benevolent side.

STYLE

Shakespeare's dramatic verse is written in iambic pentameter. An iamb is a metrical foot composed of an unaccented syllable followed by an accented one—for example, to-DAY. A pentame-

ter line consists of five feet, as at the opening of
Act IV:

if I / have TOO / ausTERE/ly PUN/ished YOU.

But *The Tempest* was written at the end of Shakespeare's career, and by the time he wrote it he had
begun introducing subtle variations into his usual
iambic pentameter. Thus, you won't find many lines
that fit the mold as perfectly as the above example.

The Tempest contains some of Shakespeare's fin-
est verse. Compared to his earlier plays, however,
it's relatively scarce in imagery. One view is that
Shakespeare had become so adept by the time he
wrote *The Tempest* that his metaphors, instead of
being rich and highly developed, dart in and out
of the verse, mere hints of images that move as
quickly as thought. An equally interesting suggestion is that *The Tempest* doesn't need as many images in its language because the play itself is an
image—you don't need metaphors for a metaphor.

An example will serve to illustrate the complexity of Shakespeare's late style. In Act I, Scene II,
as Prospero is telling Miranda about the way Antonio betrayed him, he says that his treacherous
brother,

> having both the key
> Of officer and office, set all hearts i' th' state
> To what tune pleased his ear . . .
> *(lines 83–85)*

The imagery here isn't especially vivid or sen-
suous, but the metaphor is quite complicated, and
it hinges on a pun. With the figure of a key—the
kind of key that opens a door—Prospero declares
that Antonio had control over both the dukedom

and the Duke (Prospero himself). But then the meaning of "key" changes to a musical one, as in "the key of C-sharp," and the metaphor changes to a musical one, too.

The Tempest is one of Shakespeare's romances, and as such it has a fairy-tale quality. The language of the play reflects that quality. It's stark and tragic at points, notably during the beginning storm scene and in the last two acts, when Prospero is deciding between vengeance and forgiveness, and a tragic outcome seems possible. But generally the language is among Shakespeare's loveliest and most delicate. Caliban's famous speech, "Be not afeard; the isle is full of noises" (Act III, Scene II) provides an excellent example of the language of the romance.

ELIZABETHAN ENGLISH

All languages change. Differences in pronunciation and word choice are apparent even between parents and children. If language differences can appear in one generation, it is only to be expected that the English used by Shakespeare four hundred years ago will differ markedly from the English used today. The following information on Shakespeare's language will help you understand *The Tempest*.

Mobility of Word Classes

Adjectives, nouns, and verbs were less rigidly confined to particular classes in Shakespeare's day. Adjectives were often used adverbially. In Act V, scene i, line 309, Prospero speaks of "dear-beloved" where today we would require "dearly-beloved." Adjectives could also function as nouns. In Act I, scene ii, line 329, Prospero describes "that vast of night," where a modern speaker would use "vast abyss."

Nouns were often used as verbs. Caliban complains:

> . . . here you sty me . . .
> *(I, ii, 344)*

where "sty" is the equivalent of "keep me in filthy conditions."

And verbs could occasionally function as nouns, as when "manage" is used for "management" in

> The manage of my state
> *(I, ii, 69)*

Changes in Word Meaning

The meanings of words undergo changes, a process that can be illustrated by the fact that "nice" formerly meant "wanton." Many of the words in Shakespeare still exist today, but their meanings have changed. The change may be small, as in the case of "plantation," which meant "colonization," as in

> Had I plantation of this isle, my lord
> *(II, i, 137)*

or more fundamental, so that "complexion" *(I, i, 29)* meant "outward appearance," "gaberdine" *(II, ii, 103)* meant "long, outer garment," "monstrous" *(III, iii, 31)* meant "nonhuman," "rack" *(IV, i, 156)* meant "small cloud" and "admire" *(V, i, 154)* meant "wonder at, be amazed by."

Vocabulary Loss

Words not only change their meanings, but are frequently discarded from the language. In the past, "bootless" (I, ii, 35) meant "useless," "foison" (II, i, 159) meant "abundant harvest," and "welkin" (I, ii, 4) meant "sky, heavens." The following words used in *The Tempest* are no longer current in English, but their meaning can usually be gauged from the context in which they occur.

yare *(I, i, 6)* promptly, speedily
teen *(I, ii, 64)* sorrow, trouble
coil *(I, ii, 207)* confusion
flote *(I, ii, 234)* sea
bate *(I, ii, 246)* reduce, abate
hests *(I, ii, 274)* commands
chirurgeonly *(II, i, 136)* surgeonlike
tilth *(II, i, 148)* tillage of the land
chough *(II, i, 261)* jackdaw, kind of crow
feater *(II, i, 268)* more gratefully
kibe *(II, i, 272)* chilblain, inflamed sore
inch-meal *(II, ii, 3)* inch by inch
mow *(II, ii, 9)* make faces, grimace
bombard *(II, ii, 21)* vessel for carrying liquids
deboshed *(III, ii, 25)* debauched
doit *(II, ii, 32)* small coin
scamel *(II, ii, 172)* bird, seagull
patch *(III, ii, 62)* jester, fool
freshes *(III, ii, 66)* springs of fresh water
murrain *(III, ii, 78)* disease
wezand *(III, ii, 89)* windpipe
troll *(III, ii, 115)* sing cheerfully
catch *(III, ii, 124)* song, tune
lakin *(III, iii, 1)* little lady, By Our Lady
forthrights *(III, iii, 3)* straight paths
dowle *(III, iii, 65)* small feather

bass *(III, iii, 99)* speak in deep/low tones
stover *(IV, i, 63)* hay, cattle fodder
twilled *(IV, i, 64)* woven
bosky *(IV, i, 82)* wooded
varlets *(IV, i, 170)* rogues
pard *(IV, i, 261)* leopard
pioned *(IV, ii, 64)* dug
demi-puppets *(V, i, 36)* small spirits
justle *(V, i, 158)* push, drive
mo *(V, i, 234)* more

Verbs

Shakespearean verb forms differ from modern usage in three main ways: 1. Questions and negatives could be formed without using "do/did," as when Alonso asks Gonzalo:

> Heard you this, Gonzalo?
> *(II, ii, 311)*

where today we would say: "Have you heard this?," or where Antonio states:

> . . . But I feel not
> This deity in my bosom
> *(II, i, 272)*

where modern usage demands: "I do not feel . . ." Shakespeare had the option of using the following forms **a** and **b**, whereas contemporary usage permits only **a**:

a	b
How do you look?	How look you?
How did he look?	How looked he?
You do not look well.	You look not well.
You did not look well.	You looked not well.

2. A number of past participles and past tense forms

are used that would be ungrammatical today.
Among these are:

"holp" for "helped" in

> By foul play, as thou sayest, were we heaved
> thence,
> But blessedly holp hither
>
> (I, ii, 62–3)

"forgot" for "forgotten" in

> . . . Hast thou forgot
> (I, ii, 257)

"broke" for "broken" in

> I have broke your hest to say so
> (III, i, 37)

"spoke" for "spoken" in

> Fairly spoke
> (IV, i, 31)

and "waked" and "oped" for "wakened" and
"opened" in

> . . . graves at my command
> Have waked their sleepers, oped, and let 'em
> forth
>
> (V, i, 48–9).

3. Archaic verb forms sometimes occur with "thou"
and "he/she/it":

> Thou wert but a lost monster
> (IV, i, 202)

> . . . he hath lost his fellows
> (I, ii, 418)

Pronouns

Shakespeare and his contemporaries had one extra pronoun, "thou," which could be used in addressing a person who was one's equal or social inferior. "You" was obligatory if more than one person was addressed, and this is the pronoun used by the boatswain to the courtly party:

> Do you not hear him? You mar our labour; keep
> your cabins
>
> *(I, i, 12–13)*

but it could also be used to indicate respect, as when Miranda and Ferdinand express their love for each other:

> *Mir.* Do you love me?
> *Fer.* . . . I
> Beyond all limit of what else i' th' world
> Do love, prize, honour you.
>
> *(III, i, 67ff)*

Frequently, a person in power used "thou" to a subordinate but was addressed "you" in return, as when Gonzalo and the boatswain speak:

> *Gon.* Good, yet remember whom thou hast
> aboard
> *Boat.* . . . You are a counsellor, if you can
> command these elements to silence . . .
>
> *(I, i, 19ff)*

but if "thou" was used inappropriately, it could cause grave offense.

One further pronominal reference warrants a comment. There was not a sharp distinction between "it" and "he/she" in Elizabethan English. Miranda describes Caliban:

> 'Tis a villain, sir
> *(I, ii, 311)*

and Stephano used "it" where "she" would now
be obligatory:

> Is it so brave a lass?
> *(III, ii, 101)*

Prepositions

Prepositions were less standardized in the past than
they are today, and so we find several uses in *The
Tempest* that would have to be modified in contemporary speech. Among these are "on" for "of" in

> And sucked my verdure out on it
> *(I, ii, 87)*

"to" for "for" in

> Tunis was never graced before with such a par-
> agon to their Queen
> *(II, i, 71–2)*

"of" for "from":

> . . . she was of Carthage, not of Tunis
> *(II, i, 79)*

"with" for "in":

> . . . with a twink
> *(IV, i, 43)*

and "on" for "in":

> . . . on a trice
> *(V, i, 238)*

Multiple Negation

Contemporary English requires only one negative
per statement and regards such utterances as "I
haven't none" as nonstandard. Shakespeare often

used two or more negatives for emphasis and the following occur in *The Tempest*:

> This is no mortal business nor no sound
> That the earth owes
>
> (I, ii, 409–10)

and

> Nor go neither; but you'll lie, like dogs, and yet
>   say nothing neither
>
> (III, ii, 18–19)

POINT OF VIEW

Usually it isn't productive to talk about "point of view" in a play. A novel, in contrast, has a narrator. He or she may be omniscient, standing outside the story, reading the characters' thoughts and perhaps offering some opinions of his or her own; or the narrator may be one of the characters in the story. But a play rarely has a narrator, as the various characters speak for themselves.

To an unusual degree, however, you see *The Tempest* from one character's point of view—Prospero's. Shakespeare seems to endorse Prospero's opinions: the magician may not be perfect, but most of what he says is trustworthy (except, perhaps, when he's very angry). Besides, like author and spectator, Prospero witnesses almost all of the action (and he controls most of it). When he's not there, Ariel is there in his stead, so he misses very little. He witnesses Miranda and Ferdinand's declaration of love (Act III, Scene I) and the punishment of the "three men of sin" (Act III, Scene III). Prospero doesn't *tell* the story, like an omniscient narrator; however, in the sense that he's behind the events, he *creates* it. You may feel, however, as some readers have, that this limitation in the point of view is a drawback. Because you see everything from Prospero's standpoint, it's difficult to develop real sympathy for some of the other characters. What would the play be like, for example, if you saw things through Alonso's eyes? Or Gonzalo's? It would have a very different feeling, and Prospero would certainly seem less ideal than he does as the play stands.

FORM AND STRUCTURE

The Tempest is unique among Shakespeare's mature plays in observing the classical unities of time (everything happens in one day—a matter of hours, in fact) and of place (everything happens in one locale, Prospero's island or just offshore). Critics in Shakespeare's time thought observing the unities was essential to good drama. Could Shakespeare have been sensitive to criticism, attempting in *The Tempest* to prove that he was adept at dramatic construction?

The play has been criticized, however, for lacking one of the most basic elements of good drama: tension. There's conflict, of course—between Prospero and, at one point or another, practically all the other characters—but there's not much suspense about the outcome. Prospero is in control from beginning to end. The only real question is whether he'll forgive his enemies.

The Tempest is also unusual in its division by Shakespeare into five acts, along the lines of classical Roman tragedies. Of course, we're accustomed to five-act Shakespeare, but these divisions are usually the work of later editors. Here, however, structural evidence suggests the playwright himself divided *The Tempest* into five acts.

Shakespeare's romances differ from his other comedies, with which they're often grouped, in their emphasis on the passage of time. In *The Winter's Tale*, for example, sixteen years pass between Acts III and IV. *The Tempest* differs from the other romances in that time passes not within the play—the action takes place in just a few hours—but before it. Twelve years have passed between Prospero's exile from Milan and the storm that opens the play.

The romances, as a group, share certain other characteristics. One is the gross improbability of the action. Magical things happen; the plays are almost like fairy tales. (Improbable events happen in the comedies, too, but those events are more like coincidence than magic.) Also, the character relationships, especially the love relationships, are simpler in the romances than in the other comedies. Ferdinand and Miranda's love isn't much different from that of Prince Charming and the Sleeping Beauty; it doesn't have the psychological depth that you find in Shakespeare's earlier love relationships such as Romeo and Juliet's.

Two plot elements are noteworthy in the romances. First, they share a concern with storm—a concern that gives *The Tempest* its title. Second, travel on the sea always plays a part in them. *The Tempest* begins with a voyage, and ends with the characters preparing for another one.

The Five-Act Structure

Act I: Exposition. The storm; Prospero fills Miranda in past events; introduction of Ariel and Caliban.

Act II: Rising Action. Antonio and Sebastian plot
   against Alonso; Caliban joins forces with Stephano and Trinculo.
Act III: Climax. Ferdinand and Miranda declare
   their love; Ariel charms Caliban's group into following him, and punishes the "three men of sin."
Act IV: Falling Action. The spirits' masque for Ferdinand and Miranda; Prospero and Ariel punish
   the thieves.
Act V: Conclusion. Prospero forgives his enemies.

SOURCES

The Tempest is one of a handful of Shakespearean
comedies for which we can't pinpoint the sources.
There have been some attempts to link it to a slightly
earlier German comedy *Comedia von der schönen Si-
dea*, by Jakob Ayrer (1543–1605), but the evidence
isn't convincing.

There are, however, elements within the play
that are clearly related to other documents. The
most important of these documents are a series of
pamphlets concerning the survival of some mariners in the Bermuda Islands after a tempest in 1609.
Until then, the Bermudas were popularly thought
to be inhabited by demons and fairies. The Bermuda pamphlets were published in 1610, around
the time Shakespeare was writing *The Tempest*, and
it's evident from certain similarities of phrase,
especially in the first act, that he read and remem-
bered them. It's also probable that the whole idea
of survival on a lush, remote, magical island influ-
enced his conception of *The Tempest*.

There are several speeches for which we can cite
a specific source. One is Gonzalo's fantasy (Act

II, Scene I) about governing the island; this was based on the French essayist Montaigne's "Of the Cannibals," a treatise on the American Indians, which was published in the English translation of John Florio in 1603. Prospero's farewell to his art (Act V, Scene I) adopts phrases from the Roman poet Ovid's *Metamorphoses*; Shakespeare apparently drew both on Arthur Golding's 1567 translation and on the Latin original. There are a few other details whose origins we can trace: for example, the name of the devil-god Setebos, whom Caliban and his mother worship, comes from Robert Eden's *History of Travel* (1577), where Setebos is mentioned as a devil worshipped by the Patagonians of South America.

The Play

ACT I

ACT I, SCENE I

The Tempest opens with the excitement of a raging storm at sea. The wind is howling violently, and huge waves threaten the ship. Confusion reigns on board. The ship's boatswain (the officer in charge of the deck crew) is vigorously calling out orders as he attempts to save the ship. But a group of frightened noblemen keep hounding him, making it difficult for him to do his job. You get a glimpse of Alonso, the King of Naples, the first of the nobles to speak, and later you hear that he and his son the Prince are praying below. Despite the mariners' best efforts, the storm triumphs; cries of "We split!" signal that the boat is breaking apart. As the scene ends, the men prepare to sink with their king.

NOTE: The social order In Shakespeare's day, people regarded the social hierarchy—with the king (or queen) at the top, then the nobles, and then the commoners at the bottom—as the earthly reflection of a larger "chain of being." This great hierarchy descended from God, at the top, to the lowest earthly vermin; human beings had their place between the angels and the animals. Monarchs were God's lieutenants on earth, and it was their responsibility to see that the proper order was maintained there. The tempest of this opening scene, however, turns the social order topsy-turvy. In a well-ordered world, the King would be giving directions and the seamen would be obeying them, but in the midst of a natural disaster, the order is inverted.

In the next scene, you'll learn that the social order has been inverted in another way: one of the noblemen on board, Antonio, is a usurper—a false monarch who has stolen power from a real one. In a sense, the tempest, a natural upheaval, is a symbol for this social upheaval.

Though the first scene is brief and chaotic, Shakespeare has already begun drawing character portraits. Spectators wouldn't know yet who Antonio and Sebastian are, but they'd be able to see that they're arrogant, meddlesome aristocrats who don't have the good sense to leave the boatswain alone. (To his credit, the boatswain manages to come back with a snappy response. When Sebastian curses his insolence, he retorts, "Work you, then"—Get to work!) You are also amply introduced to Gonzalo. The old councilor, though talkative, is even-tempered and optimistic. While the other nobles are panicking or praying for their lives, he manages to inject a little humor into the situation. Making a joke of the proverb "He that's born to be hanged need fear no drowning," he observes that the rough boatswain looks exactly like the kind of scoundrel who's bound for the gallows—so perhaps they're all safe from drowning. At the end of the scene, he invokes Providence—the will of a benevolent God—with the words, "The wills above be done!" Providence will form an important theme in *The Tempest*, for the shipwreck, though seemingly a disaster, will turn out to be a kind of blessing for the men on board.

ACT I, SCENE II

Lines 1–186

The scene shifts from the enchanted island where the rest of the play takes place. Prospero, scholar and magician, stands before his quarters talking with his kind-hearted daughter Miranda. She knows her father has called up the storm and she begs him to calm it, for she has spotted the ship and is terrified for whomever might be aboard.

NOTE: Observe that while Miranda addresses her father as "you," he uses the "thou" form of the second-person pronoun with her. In Elizabethan English (as in present-day French, German, and other languages), the "you" form is more formal or respectful; the "thou" form expresses familiarity.

Prospero promises Miranda that the storm hasn't harmed a hair of anybody aboard the ship. But at the moment he wants to speak to Miranda about something else: her background, about which he's so far avoided telling her. He reminds her that she wasn't quite three years old when they came to the island; because he mentions, a few lines later, that they've been there twelve years, you can estimate her age at fifteen.

Prospero tells Miranda that he was once the powerful Duke of Milan (Shakespeare puts the accent on the first syllable: MI-lan. The Italy of Shakespeare's day was not the unified nation it is today, but rather a collection of states, each of which had its own government.) Miranda, the princess, was Prospero's only child and heir. "Foul play" drove them out of Milan, but a blessing brought them to this island. (Note that the theme of divine providence is invoked again.)

The heroes of tragedy are often good men who have a fatal flaw. Although *The Tempest* is no tragedy, the Prospero who ruled Milan had just such a flaw: he loved learning too much, and it proved to be his downfall. He spent more and more time alone in study, turning the rulership of Milan over to his brother Antonio. But Antonio's head was swayed by power: he convinced himself that he was the rightful duke. Thus, he made a deal with Prospero's enemy, the King of Naples: If the King would help Antonio drive his brother out of office, then Antonio would see that Milan paid him a yearly sum of money ("annual tribute") and would make Milan, which had been a sovereign power, subservient to Naples. His plan wasn't only treacherous, it was unpatriotic. Prospero, recalling it, cringes at the thought of Milan bowing to Naples. The King of Naples accordingly raised a "treacherous army" that one midnight carried off Prospero and the child Miranda. The army didn't dare kill them, because the two were so beloved by the people; instead, they were set adrift in a rotten little boat. The one bright spot was the behavior of Gonzalo, the kindly Neapolitan councilor. He provided them with food and fresh water, and also with some "rich garments"—which may explain the existence of Prospero's magic robe, as well as the fine clothes with which, in Act IV, he tempts a band of thieves. (Antonio, the King of Naples, and Gonzalo have already appeared—though a spectator might not realize it—in the opening of the shipboard scene.)

You may find Prospero's narrative a little difficult to follow at first. These memories excite and anger him, thus his sentence structure isn't as clean and precise as it would be if he were calmer. His excitement is probably also one reason that he keeps asking Miranda if she's listening, though it's perfectly obvious that she's very attentive.

NOTE: The classical unities Prospero's long speech provides the background information you need in order to follow the rest of the story. But it would have been almost as easy, and much more dramatic, for Shakespeare to have included one or two early scenes actually showing these events. By giving the narrative to Prospero, he observes what were known as the classical unities.

The ancient Greek philosopher Aristotle had observed that most tragedies confine themselves to "a single revolution of the sun." Renaissance critics turned his observation into a strict rule, insisting that not only must the action of a play be restricted to a single day, it should remain in a single place as well. If you're familiar with Shakespeare's other plays, you'll know that he wasn't impressed by these so-called rules; in fact, he was criticized for not adhering to them. Some scholars believe that in composing *The Tempest* along such strictly unified lines (the play takes place within a few hours and everything happens on Prospero's island, or just offshore), Shakespeare was showing his critics how rigorous he could be if he wanted to. But it's equally possible that Shakespeare didn't care at all about critical theory—that he constructed *The Tempest* as he did simply because it suited the effect for which he was striving.

Prospero ends his tale by informing Miranda that his enemies are now on the shore of his island, and that he must act swiftly to make his good luck secure. Miranda promptly, and rather unexpectedly, falls asleep. Possibly she sleeps because it suits Prospero's purposes: he wants her out of the way so he can talk privately with Ariel. But there's also a chance that Shakespeare is poking fun at himself here, as if to say, "I know how tedious all this background is getting. Look, even the actors can't keep their eyes open."

Lines 187–304

Perhaps you noticed that Prospero, in his narrative, moved from a rather stark and tragic realism, as he recalled his downfall, to the almost fairy-tale tone with which he described the journey to the blessed island. The texture of the play has changed, too. It began with a terrifying and realisitc storm; now, as Prospero summons the spirit Ariel, it moves into the realm of delightful fantasy.

Ariel is described in the opening cast of characters as "an airy spirit." He's all lightness, speed, fire, and music; there's nothing bodily about him. In fact, you can only call him "he" for the sake of convenience, since he can assume a female form as easily as a male one.

Prospero asks whether Ariel has created the tempest he was commanded to create, and Ariel replies with a description of his mischief. Turning himself into fire, he danced in the guise of flames all around the ship, terrifying the men. All the noblemen on board jumped into the sea, but Ariel has seen to it that they're all safely ashore; in fact, their clothes are even fresher than before. Ariel has separated them into groups; the King's son, Ferdinand (who was the first to jump overboard), is by himself. The ship is hidden in a "deep nook" in the harbor; the sailors are below deck, sleeping a sleep that's half exhaustion, half enchantment.

NOTE: "The still-vexed Bermoothes" When Ariel mentions going to "fetch dew" from the Bermuda Islands, it's the only allusion to the Bermudas in the play, but it isn't coincidental. (The spelling "Bermoothes" imitates the Spanish pronunciation of the name.) In 1609 a group of British ships had set sail for the new Jamestown colony in Virginia; one of the ships, separated from the others in a storm, ran aground in the Bermuda Islands. But the report that first reached England was that the ship had sunk, and that the crew was dead. Thus, when the English public learned the next year that the seamen had survived after all, the news caused quite a stir. Several pamphlets about the adventure were published, and Shakespeare, who was writing *The Tempest* at about that time, apparently read them attentively, since some of them seem to have provided a source for certain descriptions in the play. The storm scene at the outset, for example, echoes phrases from the Bermuda pamphlets. Ariel's description of his fiery antics recalls a description of "Sea-fire" in one of the pamphlets.

The safety of the shipwrecked men on the lush Bermuda Islands caught the imagination of the English public for another reason as well. Until then, there was a great deal of superstition surrounding the islands. They were associated in the public mind with winds and enchantments, with fairies and demons. That's why Ariel calls them "still-vexed," ever-tormented. (In our day there's talk about the treacherous Bermuda Triangle, where ships and airplanes have disappeared.) The disaster that turns out to be a blessing is, as you will see, an important theme in *The Tempest*. The theme has already been mentioned once: in Prospero's speech describing the way he and Miranda reached the fortunate island, "By providence divine."

The idea of an exotic island, inhabited by fairies appealed to Shakespeare's imagination. Geographically, however, Prospero's island is nowhere near the Bermudas; it's somewhere in the Mediterranean Sea. You know this because you learn, in Act II, that the King of Naples' fleet was returning to Italy from North Africa when the tempest struck.

Prospero is pleased with Ariel's report, and he tells him that the next four hours—from two until six—will be of the highest importance. But Ariel isn't eager for more work. He reminds Prospero of a promise he made to take a year off Ariel's term of service. You may be surprised that Prospero is angered by Ariel's request. The magician suddenly becomes threatening. He makes Ariel recall the terrible punishment from which he once saved him. Years earlier, Ariel had been the servant of the "foul witch" Sycorax, who was banished to the island from her native Algiers "For mischiefs manifold, and sorceries terrible." (When Prospero calls her a "blue-eyed hag," he's referring to the color of her eyelids, not her eyes. Blue eyelids were considered a sign of pregnancy, and when Sycorax arrived at the island she was pregnant with the monster Caliban—whom you'll shortly meet.)

Sycorax's commands were so horrible that Ariel refused to carry them out. As a punishment, she imprisoned him in a cloven (split) pine tree, and he remained there, in groaning agony, for a dozen years, during which time Sycorax died. Eventually Prospero arrived on the island, opened the pine with a magic stronger than Sycorax's, and released Ariel—on the condition that Ariel work for him.

Sycorax's punishment seems especially terrible because Ariel, the air spirit, is the very essence of freedom. By the same token, it may strike you as wrong that he should have to be anybody's servant. Thus, Prospero's rage at Ariel's wish for liberty seems overly harsh, and when he threatens to imprison Ariel in an oak tree for another twelve years, you may think he's gone too far. (The horrified Ariel quickly promises to do whatever he's told.)

You should keep several factors in mind, however. The first is that the following hours are very important indeed. Prospero has already told Miranda that if he doesn't seize his good fortune now, it will desert him forever. A second, deeper factor concerns what Prospero has learned from past experience. He lost Milan by being a weak, inattentive ruler; thus, he keeps a firm (but not cruel) control over his island domain. Finally, it was part of fairy folklore that anyone who controlled the spirits had to keep a careful eye on them, because their natural inclination was toward freedom, not work.

But just when Prospero is starting to seem tyrannical, he becomes kindly—as if his harshness had been a joke. Once he's assured of Ariel's service, he promises Ariel that if he performs well, he'll set him free in two days. Ariel is delighted. Prospero orders him to assume female shape—"a nymph o' th' sea"—and to make himself invisible to everyone but Prospero.

Lines 305–374

Prospero wakens Miranda, then calls Caliban, the monster son of Sycorax. Miranda hates Caliban ("'Tis a villain, sir,/I do not love to look on"), but

Prospero reminds her that they need him: he builds their fire, fetches their wood, and performs similar menial tasks.

Caliban is described in the opening cast of characters as "a salvage [that is, savage] and deformed slave." Prospero keeps him imprisoned in a kind of rock-den. His first words, a complaint from off-stage, are typical: "There's wood enough within." He knows he's being called to work, and he doesn't feel like it. Caliban is sullen, insolent, uncooperative, and lazy. When Prospero says that he was "got by the devil himself/Upon thy wicked dam," he's probably referring to the actual circumstances of Caliban's birth rather than simply insulting him. The monster's mother, you remember, was the witch Sycorax; his father was apparently a demon.

At first Caliban seems sympathetic even though he's bad-tempered. Prospero has nothing but nasty words for him ("poisonous slave," "lying slave" and so forth), and when Caliban resists his authority, Prospero is even harsher than he was with Ariel. Prospero threatens to set "urchins" (goblins) on him, who will pinch him so cruelly he'll look like a honeycomb. Caliban delivers a speech that makes him seem even more cruelly victimized, claiming that the island, which once belonged to him, has been stolen from him. When Prospero first arrived on the island, he treated Caliban kindly, teaching him language and petting him. In return, Caliban acquainted him with his wide knowledge of the island. Now he curses himself for having helped Prospero, since Prospero has made him a slave and imprisoned him. Poor Caliban can't even roam the island that was once all his own. Consider the plight of the seventeenth-century American Indians if you want to show some sympathy for Caliban.

One of the qualities that made Shakespeare a supreme dramatist was his profound understanding of, and sympathy for, his characters—even his villains. For the moment, Shakespeare takes you into the monster's mind and shows you the world from *his* point of view; he gives Caliban a fair chance to speak for himself.

Prospero retorts that Caliban is a liar, and that what works with him is whipping, not kindness. He had raised and educated the monster with great kindness—which Caliban repaid by trying to rape Miranda. Caliban, on being reminded of his crime, cries, "O ho, O ho! Would't had been done!" and he basks, remorseless, in the vision of an island populated by baby Calibans. Suddenly you glimpse Caliban's true nature.

You should keep in mind that English citizens of Shakespeare's day held very different ideas about the social order than we do. Notions of equality and democracy were completely foreign, even upsetting, to them. They believed in a strict hierarchy, from king down to commoner, and they believed that the world was ordered that way because that was how God had ordained it. Kings ruled by divine right, a right bestowed on them by God. Aristocrats weren't just lucky men and women who had the benefits of wealth, education, and comfort—they enjoyed these blessings because their noble natures deserved them. Similarly, laborers toiled because physical work suited their lower, earthier natures. Such ideas may strike you as silly

and superstitious, but they were fundamental to
the Elizabethan picture of an ordered society.

Caliban is a slave *by nature.* (Prospero calls him
"slave" six times in this brief section.) Servitude is
what he's fit for. The attempt to educate him for
something better and nobler has only perverted
him—a fact Prospero has learned the hard way.
No wonder Prospero sometimes appears so stern,
even authoritarian. Caliban represents his second
failure as a ruler. (Losing Milan to his brother Antonio was his first.)

In many ways, Caliban is central to the structure
of *The Tempest.* Shakespeare has set up implied
contrasts between the monster and several other
characters. For example, Caliban is described in
the cast of characters as "deformed," and his ugliness—which is the outward reflection of his inner
vileness—contrasts sharply with Miranda's beauty,
which is in turn the emblem of her beautiful nature. Prospero has taken great pains to educate his
daughter:

> . . . here
> Have I, thy schoolmaster, made thee more profit
> Than other princess' can, that have more time
> For vainer hours, and tutors not so careful.

Miranda benefits greatly from her education because she has a noble nature to begin with. On the
other hand, the main benefit Caliban has reaped
from learning to speak is that he's become an expert at cursing. Education has only made him into
a malcontent concerning his low position. He may
have been born to serve, but learning has made
him hate serving.

Miranda isn't the only character with whom Shakespeare contrasts Caliban. As the former ruler of the island, and the representative of "nature," Caliban is a counterpart to the current ruler, Prospero, the representative of "art" or learning. Caliban is even more obviously Ariel's precise opposite. Ariel is "an airy spirit"—light, speedy, intelligent. But almost the first words Prospero speaks to Caliban are "Thou earth, thou!" Caliban may be viewed as heavy, earthbound, stupid—everything that Ariel isn't. Whereas Ariel is pure spirit, Caliban is all body, and thus, all uncontrolled appetite. He doesn't control his desires because he can't. (Hence his attempt to rape Miranda.) Later he'll turn out to be a drunkard as well.

You'll see another contrast with Caliban in Ferdinand, the King of Naples' son. Ferdinand, like Miranda the child of royalty, has a noble nature. Among his many virtues is chastity, or, more broadly, self-control. Caliban, all appetite, will never know the meaning of self-control.

Lines 375–503

Ariel returns singing, invisible to everyone but Prospero (this effect was probably accomplished in Shakespeare's day by having the actor wear a special robe signaling invisibility). Ferdinand, son of the King of Naples, closely resembles a fairy-tale prince—handsome, brave, and noble. Shakespeare never really develops an in-depth portrait of his character. (Similarly, he doesn't develop Miranda much, beyond making her charming and virginal—a fairy-tale princess.)

Ferdinand had been weeping over what he

thought was the death of his father when this strange music came creeping by him. It calmed both him and the storm, and Ferdinand followed it almost against his will.

Ariel's second song, even lovelier than his first (and more understandable), describes the "sea-change" of a drowned man whose eyes turn to pearls and whose bones turn to coral. Sure that the words concern his father's drowning, Ferdinand decides that the music must be the work of spirits—"no mortal business." Prospero spots the young man and points him out to Miranda.

NOTE: Prospero's words are, "The fringèd curtains of thine eyes advance/And say what thou seest yond." These lines have been the center of a lively controversy for centuries, with such famous literary names as Alexander Pope and Samuel Taylor Coleridge lining up on opposite sides. Pope's followers think the phrasing is too pompous, since it's nothing more than an overblown way of saying, "Look what's coming." Coleridge's followers defend Shakespeare, arguing that the words are appropriate to Prospero's general solemnity, and that Prospero obviously wants Miranda's first view of Ferdinand to make a strong impression on her. It's a small but unresolved issue, and you'll have to read the lines several times in context to decide which argument you favor.

When Miranda sees Ferdinand, she's so overwhelmed by his good looks that she decides he must be a spirit, or even a god (a "thing divine").

Ferdinand has the same reaction: is Miranda a goddess? Prospero observes that everything is proceeding according to his plan: "They have changed eyes", that is, they've fallen in love at first sight (another fairy-tale convention). Prospero is so delighted that he promises the invisible Ariel he'll set him free for this.

But Prospero doesn't show his pleasure to the young lovers. Ferdinand, surprised to hear Miranda speaking his own language, tells her that he's "the best," the highest-ranking, of the people who speak it. Prospero challenges him: What would the King of Naples say if he heard that statement? The King of Naples *does* hear, Ferdinand replies, because Ferdinand himself is the King of Naples. (Remember, Ferdinand thinks his father has drowned.)

NOTE: Ferdinand's statement that the Duke of Milan (Antonio) and his son went down with the ship is a mystery, because it's the only mention in the play of Antonio's son. Scholars have offered various explanations: perhaps the reference is a holdover from an earlier version of the play; perhaps at this point in the writing Shakespeare hadn't decided on all the character relationships. Because the statement gives Prospero an opening for a witty response, it's possible that Shakespeare left it in the play simply because he didn't want to cut a good line.

Miranda is shocked at her father's harshness; she's never seen him behave so unpleasantly.

Prospero explains in an aside that if he doesn't make it difficult for Ferdinand to win Miranda, Ferdinand might not value her highly enough. Do you think this is a convincing explanation? Keep in mind, at least, that you're in the realm of fairy tale here. It's also probably worth remembering that Shakespeare had two daughters of his own. He must have understood Prospero's mixed feelings at seeing his young daughter leaving the nest— even though she's leaving it for a fine young man.

NOTE: "Aside"   You'll encounter this stage direction frequently. It indicates that a line is to be spoken secretively—either to another character on-stage (for example, when Prospero speaks to Ariel out of Miranda and Ferdinand's hearing), or directly to the audience (Caliban's lament that he must obey Prospero because his magic is so powerful). Asides to the audience are particularly useful for letting spectators in on a character's thoughts.

To Miranda's horror, Prospero grows even more belligerent. He accuses Ferdinand of trying to steal his island, and he threatens to imprison him. Finally he drives the young man to anger. Ferdinand draws his sword, but before he can use it Prospero freezes him with a charm. Ferdinand's action tells you that he's brave, but his bravery is no match for Prospero's magic.

Miranda begs her father to be merciful. Ferdinand, for his part, is ready for hardship, even imprisonment, as long as he can glimpse Miranda once a day. (Again, his declaration has a storybook

quality.) The act closes with Prospero maintaining
his facade of harshness but secretly whispering his
delight, and promises of freedom, to Ariel.

NOTE: Beauty It isn't unusual for storybook
characters like Ferdinand and Miranda to be at-
tractive, but you may be wondering why Shakespeare places so much emphasis on their appearance. Isn't there more to a person than good looks?
As a matter of fact, it was commonly believed in
Shakespeare's day that physical beauty was the
outward reflection of moral beauty. After all, according to the Bible, God created man in his own
image. Ugliness was believed to be evidence of
some kind of inward evil. (See *Richard III* for clear
evidence of this theory.) Thus Caliban, with his
low nature, is ugly and deformed. His mother, the
witch Sycorax, was "with age and envy/Grown into
a hoop." Throughout the play, physical beauty is
linked with moral beauty.

ACT II

ACT II, SCENE I

Lines 1–188
Attention now focuses on Ferdinand's father, the
King of Naples, and the other nobles you met in
the storm scene. Kindly old Gonzalo—the same
good councilor who provided Prospero and Miranda with food, fresh water, and clothing when
they were set adrift twelve years ago—is trying to
cheer King Alonso. But Alonso is in no mood for

words of comfort; his first line is "Prithee, peace"—
Please be quiet.

Gonzalo is supported in his efforts at optimism
by two lords—Adrian and Francisco. They're no
match, however, for two nasty, cynical noblemen
who keep interrupting their cheerful talk with jeers
and insults. One of these mockers, Antonio, is
Prospero's brother, who drove Prospero and Miranda out of Milan and usurped Prospero's dukedom. The other cynic, Sebastian, is Alonso's
brother, who is no more likable than Antonio.

NOTE: Pairing   You might pause here to consider
with what symmetry Shakespeare has cast *The
Tempest*. Almost every character has a counterpart.
Prospero and Alonso, rightful rulers as well as
fathers, form one pair; their wicked brothers, Antonio and Sebastian, form another; their children,
Miranda and Ferdinand, form a third. Adrian and
Francisco, two lords, both have bit parts. Ariel and
Caliban, the two fantastic beings on Prospero's island, are counterparts and opposites. In Act II,
Scene II, you'll meet Trinculo and Stephano, two
low-born clowns who survive the shipwreck.
Among the major characters, only Gonzalo stands
alone outside these symmetries; he has no counterpart. Why do you think this is the case? You
might say he's the exception that proves the rule,
though in fact sometimes Gonzalo is paired with
Alonso, as the voice of optimism countering Alonso's voice of pessimism.

As Antonio and Sebastian continue their sarcastic comments and stupid jokes, you may find them more and more irritating. Here Shakespeare gives you an example of the way a person's temperament shapes his perceptions. To the optimistic Gonzalo, the grass on the island is "lush and lusty . . . how green!" But to the sour Antonio it looks "tawny"—dried up by the sun. (Can you give a similar example from your own experience of how two people saw the same incident in two different ways?) Gonzalo is amazed that their clothing, instead of being stained with salt water, seems clean and fresh. (Recall that in Act I, Scene II, Ariel told Prospero that his magic had made the men's garments "fresher than before.") However, Antonio and Sebastian don't seem convinced.

Gonzalo and his tormentors argue rather trivially for several lines. Gonzalo identifies the city of Tunis, from which the King's fleet was returning, with the ancient city of Carthage. In fact, the ruins of Carthage are quite close to Tunis. But Antonio and Sebastian belittle him as if he were an idiot for saying so. When Gonzalo refers to the "widow Dido," they hoot at that too; apparently because people don't usually think of Dido, the passionate lover of Aeneas in Virgil's epic *The Aeneid*, as a widow, even though she was one. The whole passage is difficult to follow, and scholars still aren't completely sure what all the characters are talking about here. But the gist is clear: Sebastian and Antonio are mocking the old man for no good reason.

Finally the King has tolerated enough. He complains that he doesn't feel like being cheered; grief-stricken, he laments the death of his son Ferdinand. Francisco offers some comfort: he says he saw Ferdinand swimming strongly over the water, and there's every reason to believe he reached the shore. Nevertheless, Alonso still doesn't believe that Ferdinand might be alive.

Sebastian doesn't even try to comfort his brother. Instead, he's cruel enough to rub salt in his wounds. The whole disaster, he says, is the King's fault. The storm struck while their fleet was on its way home to Naples from North Africa, where they had all attended the wedding of the King's daughter Claribel to the King of Tunis. Sebastian reminds the King that he (Sebastian) and many others—including Claribel herself—opposed the marriage. They didn't want her marrying someone from so remote a land. Alonso had refused to yield, however, and his stubbornness, Sebastian tells him, was the real cause of the present catastrophe.

Gonzalo reproaches Sebastian for talking to a grieving man that way. Still determined to cheer the King, the old councilor decides to entertain him with a fantasy of what he'd do if he had "plantation of this isle"—that is, colonization rights. (But Sebastian and Antonio make another inane joke—that Gonzalo would plant it with briars and weeds.)

Gonzalo's odd little speech envisions an island without money, jobs, or farming; without ownership, inheritance, or weapons. An innocent, uncivilized population would live off the fat of a fertile land, an Eden. His fantasy of an ideal society is a far cry from the highly organized monarchies of seventeenth-century Europe.

NOTE: Montaigne   Gonzalo's speech is one of the few spots in *The Tempest* for which we are sure of Shakespeare's source: a piece of writing called "On

the Cannibals" by the great French essayist Michel
de Montaigne (1533–1592). Montaigne's essay was
published in an English translation in 1603, and
Gonzalo's speech echoes phrases from it so closely
that it's certain Shakespeare had read it.

Montaigne idealized primitive, "natural" socie-
ties at the expense of the highly "artificial" social
organization of European monarchies, with their
crime, poverty, and vice. Shakespeare's purpose
in quoting him, however, is less clear. Gonzalo,
trying to divert the King, is speaking half-jokingly.
But is he half-serious too? The Shakespeare who
created Caliban certainly hasn't idealized brute nature. On the other hand, like Montaigne, he's evidently concerned with the corrupting influence of
civilization, because he includes Antonio and Sebastian in the play. These two men, you could argue, are worse than Caliban; the monster behaves
according to his low nature, but in their corruption
they've allowed their higher nature to be perverted. How seriously Shakespeare intends Gonzalo's speech is a point you'll have to decide about
later, after gathering evidence from the rest of the
play. Watch for two themes: the benevolence of
nature, and the corrupting force of civilization.

Patient as he is, Gonzalo doesn't enjoy the jeers
of Antonio and Sebastian. He keeps his temper,
but he leaves no doubt as to his opinion of their
"wit."

Lines 189–331

Ariel enters, still invisible and playing magical music that immediately puts Gonzalo, Adrian, and

Francisco into an enchanted sleep. As Alonso grows drowsy too, Sebastian encourages him to sleep and soothe his grief. Antonio promises that they'll guard the King's safety while he dozes—an outrageous lie, in view of the murderous scheme he's about to hatch with Sebastian. Ariel leaves, and Sebastian and Antonio wonder why they haven't become sleepy too. As you'll see, leaving them awake is part of Prospero's plan.

With the others out of the way, Antonio draws Sebastian into a plot to kill the King and take the crown for himself. (If you've read *Macbeth*, what resemblance do you find between Antonio and the scheming Lady Macbeth?) Sebastian only gradually perceives his meaning. Antonio tells the King's brother that he has a great opportunity here, if he'll only seize it. The King is asleep, defenseless; Ferdinand, who would inherit the crown if anything happened to his father, has surely drowned, despite Gonzalo's optimism. Ferdinand's sister Claribel, to whom the crown would belong after Ferdinand's death, is so far away in Tunis that for all practical purposes she's out of the picture. Antonio's style is elevated, but his meaning is simple and brutal: if Sebastian murders his brother as he sleeps, he can take the crown for himself—just as Antonio stole the crown of his own brother, Prospero.

Antonio's reasoning may sound logical to someone who's ready to be convinced, but a closer examination will reveal its falsity. Look at these sleeping lords, Antonio says; if they were dead, they'd be no worse off than they are right now. Besides, Sebastian could rule Naples just as well as Alonso. Furthermore, murdering the talkative

Gonzalo would be no loss to anybody. Antonio reminds Sebastian of his own crime against Prospero; just see how he's benefited from it, he says.

Sebastian's brief reply is straightforward: what about Antonio's conscience? Antonio assures him that his conscience doesn't even bother him as much as a kibe (a cold sore) on his foot would—less, in fact, because he would feel the sore, but he doesn't feel guilt. He tells the hesitant Sebastian that he'll murder the King at once if Sebastian will draw his sword beside him and kill loyal Gonzalo. The rest of the lords, he promises him, won't cause any problem—they'll support whoever holds the power.

Sebastian reaches a firm resolution: he'll do it. And for helping him this way, he'll free Antonio from the annual tribute that Alonso exacted for helping Antonio get rid of Prospero. If Antonio has any motive beyond sheer wickedness for urging Sebastian into the scheme, this is probably it. The two villains prepare to draw their swords, but the nervous Sebastian hesitates again, and they pause for a moment to discuss the matter further.

NOTE: Reenactment When Shakespeare decided to observe the classical unities in *The Tempest*, he sacrificed a great dramatic possibility. Antonio's plot against Prospero, which is central to the drama, would have supplied some exciting scenes. Moreover, by not staging them, Shakespeare risked not having his audience see how villainous Antonio really was. It's one thing to hear about a crime, but another to see it being planned and carried out. Therefore, by having Antonio mastermind this plot against Alonso—a plot that's almost identical to his earlier crime against Prospero—Shakespeare portrays Antonio as a usurper without having to spread the action of the play over twelve years. He even manages to create a little suspense—though not a great deal, since you'll shortly learn that everything is proceeding according to Prospero's plan.

Prospero has foreseen the danger to his old friend Gonzalo, just as he's foreseen Sebastian and Antonio's scheme. Ariel reenters and awakens Gonzalo the same way he had put him to sleep: with music. This time there's nothing vague about his song: it's a clear warning of danger. When Gonzalo opens his eyes to see Sebastian and Antonio with their swords drawn, he cries out, waking the King and the other lords.

Caught red-handed, the two villains have to invent a story. Sebastian starts rattling that he heard a noise like bulls or lions—evidently he hasn't gotten his story straight yet. Antonio chimes in that the noise was terrible. Alonso seems slightly suspicious ("I heard nothing"), but Gonzalo admits that he heard something too, though it was more like humming than roaring. Gonzalo seems ready to accept their tale if for no other reason than that he doesn't like being suspicious. Reassuring the King once more that Ferdinand must be alive somewhere on the island, they go off searching for him, while Ariel leaves to report to Prospero.

ACT II, SCENE II

On another part of the island, Caliban is at one of his chores, hauling firewood; as usual, he's cursing Prospero with every plague he can think of. He isn't worried about the spirits overhearing him because he knows they won't torment him unless Prospero orders them to. Caliban reveals their pet tortures: they pinch him, throw him in the mud, lead him astray with magic lights, turn into apes that grimace and bite him, or into hedge-hogs that prick his feet, or into snakes that wind around him. Then he sees Trinculo and mistakes him for one of Prospero's spirits come to punish him for working too slowly. He falls flat (there are no trees to hide behind) in the hope that the "spirit" won't notice him.

Trinculo, another survivor of the storm, is a jester from Alonso's court. After enduring the terror of the storm, he's still nervous about the weather. It looks like a new tempest is brewing, but he doesn't see any trees or bushes to shelter him. He sees only Caliban, and he doesn't know what to make of him. The monster smells as bad as an old fish, but he seems more like an inhabitant of the island struck dead by lightning. (Caliban, frightened of the "spirit," is lying very still.) Trinculo reflects that in England, Caliban could make his fortune: people would gladly pay a high price to behold such a marvel. Indeed, as Shakespeare knew, the English were great fans of side-shows.

NOTE: At the time Shakespeare was writing *The Tempest*, American Indians were a popular curiosity in England. They were brought over to be exhibited, but after suffering abuse they rarely lived to return home—thus, perhaps, Trinculo's reference to "a dead Indian."

Trinculo is a jester to Alonso, and he functions in the play as a clown, too. Shakespeare hasn't made him convincingly Italian; after all, he makes topical jokes about England. Note the way he uses images of drinking. The black cloud he spots looks like "a foul bombard"—a large leather jug—"that would shed his liquor"; he'll have to wait until "the dregs of the storm" are past. At this point he isn't drunk (his friend Stephano is the drunkard), but before long he'll be reeling around the stage. In any case, though he dislikes Caliban's looks, the approaching storm convinces him to crawl under Caliban's gaberdine (cloak) for protection.

Stephano, described in the cast of characters as "a drunken butler", wanders in at this point. He too was on the King's ship, and like Trinculo he thinks he's the only survivor. He stumbles around, bellowing a song about dying on dry land. It suddenly strikes him that this is hardly an appropriate song, in view of the fact that his friends have all drowned. So he takes another swig and launches into a lewd song about a woman who doesn't like sailors.

Caliban, meanwhile, is terrified of Trinculo, who's crawled under his cloak: "Do not torment me!" he cries. Stephano hears Caliban's voice, then notices the four legs (Caliban's and Trinculo's) jutting out from the cloak, and decides that he's stumbled on some kind of talking monster. It occurs to him, as it had to Trinculo, that a marvel like this could make his fortune at home.

Caliban, who still thinks he's being punished by a spirit, promises, "I'll bring my wood home faster." Stephano decides that Caliban must be having some kind of fit, and he offers the monster his favorite remedy: a swig of wine. Caliban is wary, but Stephano assures him he's a friend.

Trinculo, meanwhile, has heard Stephano's voice, and believing that Stephano drowned with the others, he decides devils must be at work. Stephano, on hearing Trinculo's voice, is even more confused: the monster seems to have not only four legs but two voices as well. They talk, and finally he drags Trinculo out with an obscene joke about Trinculo's being the dung ("siege") of a monster ("mooncalf").

Trinculo is so delighted to see his friend that he embraces him a little too energetically. Stephano, whose stomach is queasy from too much drink, asks him to stop. These two clowns form a sorry spectacle, but Caliban is convinced they're gods. After all, Stephano has given him "celestial liquor," and so he kneels to him.

Stephano, it turns out, floated to safety on (appropriately) "a butt of sack"—a keg of wine. His repeated oath, "by this bottle," is a drunkard's joke. But Caliban takes it seriously, and he offers to swear "upon that bottle" to serve Stephano. Trinculo and Stephano pay no attention to him at first. They're more excited about the butt of sack Stephano managed to save.

When they do turn to Caliban, the innocent monster wants to know if they dropped from heaven. Taking advantage of his trustfulness, Stephano claims to be the man in the moon. (In fact, the early European explorers told lies very much like this to the innocent Indians.) In any case, Stephano is delighted to have anyone admiring him. He accepts Caliban's services and gives him more wine. Trinculo, in contrast, is disgusted with Caliban's gullibility as well as his increasing tipsiness, and he's suddenly embarrassed that he feared the monster at first.

Caliban begs Stephano to let him kiss his foot, and he promises to show them all the nooks and crannies of the island—exactly as he had done twelve years earlier for Prospero. He's so delighted at the idea of escaping Prospero that he offers to catch fish for Stephano and to fetch his wood. Notice that the idea of slavery itself doesn't bother him, because he's a natural slave. All he wants is a new master.

NOTE: It's curious that while Stephano and Trinculo speak in prose, Caliban's speech is beautiful poetry. The jester and the drunken butler are ordinary men—funny, but contemptible. Caliban may be a monster, but he isn't *merely* brutal. He's a fairy-tale monster, and the beauty of his language describes his wonderful and magical nature. Do you know of another less than admirable Shakespearean character who also delivers some potent and moving lines?

Stephano decides that, because the real King has drowned, he is now the king of the island. He turns his bottle over to Trinculo, and they head off to refill it. Caliban, now thoroughly drunk, leads the way, singing and howling in joy at his new "freedom."

ACT III

ACT III, SCENE I

The action returns to Prospero's part of the island. Ferdinand enters, carrying a log. Although Ferdinand was born a prince, Prospero has him hauling firewood, which is usually the slave Caliban's task. Because this scene immediately follows the Caliban-Trinculo-Stephano farce, the shift in tone from low comic to elevated is extremely striking. While Caliban curses and complains about his chores, Ferdinand performs his task with joy, as he explains in his opening soliloquy. (A soliloquy is a form of thinking aloud—a monologue addressed directly to the audience.) Some sports, Ferdinand reflects, are painfully strenuous, but we take part in them because the fun outweighs the pain. By the same token, chores which under other circumstances would be disgusting to someone so high-born are a pleasure because he's doing them in order to win Miranda. She's easily worth the toil, though her father is "composed of harshness." Miranda has wept to watch Ferdinand engage in such base labor; but thinking of her, he says, makes the work easy.

Ferdinand's task is appropriate to the fairy-tale aspect of his character: Prospero has ordered him to remove a thousand logs and pile them up. This kind of feat is typical of legends that were old by the time Shakespeare wrote *The Tempest*. In older versions, the young man being tested had to chop the wood, plow the ground, and reap the harvest all in one day.

NOTE: "Most busiest when I do it." Scholars have spent centuries trying to decipher this line. *The Tempest*, written about 1611, was first published in 1623 in the First Folio, the famous first collected edition of Shakespeare's plays. There the line reads: "Most busie lest, when I doe it." Since that time, a number of conjectures have been offered. One is that the word should be "busieliest," meaning "most busily" (an odd formation, but it has parallels elsewhere in late Shakespeare). Another is that the line was supposed to read "Most busiest when idlest," but some letters were dropped off in the process of printing, and the printer then patched the line up incorrectly. Other explanations have also been suggested. Editors of Shakespeare often have to deal with this type of difficulty. Because spelling wasn't standardized in Shakespeare's day, and because printers were often careless, there are a number of lines in the plays where we can't be certain we're reading what Shakespeare actually wrote. Fortunately, these difficulties are usually minor; in any case, Ferdinand's meaning here seems relatively clear. Beginning with "I forget," he's reflecting that in pausing to think aloud this way, he's forgetting to continue his labors, even though thoughts of Miranda make those labors pleasant.

Miranda enters and urges Ferdinand to rest, since her father is busy studying and won't stir for the next three hours. But Miranda is wrong: Prospero is secretly watching the two young lovers. Miranda says she wishes that lightning had burned the logs during the tempest, so poor Ferdinand wouldn't have to stack them now. Creating a beautiful metaphor of the resin they'll exude when they finally do burn, she says they'll "weep for having wearied you."

Ferdinand won't stop, however, even when Miranda offers to work in his place. (A princess aiding her toiling prince was another feature of old legends.) They argue charmingly, and Prospero sees how deeply in love Miranda is.

Ferdinand doesn't even know Miranda's name, and when she tells him (even though her father had told her not to), he cries, "Admired Miranda!" This is another example of Shakespeare's puns, for the word "admire" comes from the Latin for "to wonder at"; "Miranda" means "wonderful." (Recall that when Ferdinand first saw Miranda, in Act I, Scene II, he addressed her, "O you wonder!") Ferdinand says he's known many women, but they each had some flaw. But not Miranda: she's perfect and peerless.

Miranda answers, modestly, that unlike Ferdinand she's inexperienced. She can't compare herself to other women, because she doesn't know any. For that matter, she doesn't know any men, either, except for her father and now Ferdinand. But she knows she wants no other man than Ferdinand.

Ferdinand admits that as royalty he would ordinarily detest this kind of labor. Because his heart has made him Miranda's slave, however, he can bear it patiently. Miranda very simply asks if he loves her; his reply is such an ecstatic "yes" that it makes her cry. Prospero, still watching, is delighted.

Miranda is weeping, she says, because she feels so unworthy. Because she wants to be simple, not sly, she asks him straightforwardly if he will marry her. She also promises to be his "maid" if he refuses, with a pun on "maid" as both "virgin" (because she won't marry anybody else) and "servant." Ferdinand, of course, is as eager to marry her as a slave is to be free—an appropriate comparison, considering his present bondage. Thus, they part happily.

Prospero, left alone onstage, reflects that though he can't be as happy as the lovers, he couldn't be any happier than he is. Still, there's much to be done to complete his plan.

NOTE: Reconciliation over generations   Prospero and Alonso are old enemies, as you know from Prospero's reminiscences in Act I, Scene II. Now their children, Miranda and Ferdinand, have fallen in love. The notion that a younger generation can heal the rifts between their parents is an element in several of Shakespeare's later plays. It may also remind you of one of the earlier plays in which the tragic love of Romeo and Juliet ultimately brings together their feuding families, the Montagues and the Capulets.

ACT III, SCENE II

In another sharp contrast, a delicate and serious exchange is now followed by some broad slapstick humor, including a barrage of comic puns.

Caliban, Stephano, and Trinculo are all roaring

drunk at this point. Stephano commands the others to drink up. Trinculo observes that if the other inhabitants of the island (Caliban has told them about Prospero and Miranda) have brains like theirs, then "the state totters"—a pun on their drunken staggering.

Stephano is swaggering as usual, claiming that he swam "five-and-thirty leagues" (around 120 land miles) to reach the shore. He offers to make Caliban his standard-bearer, or flag-carrier, at which Trinculo cracks that he'd be an unfit standard because he's too drunk to *stand*. He'd make a better lieutenant, "if you list." This is yet another pun: the phrase means "if you wish," but Stephano is listing like a ship—tilting drunkenly to the side.

As for Caliban, he's drunk so much wine that at first he seems barely able to talk. When he finally does, he's still fawning on Stephano. Earlier he'd begged to kiss Stephano's foot; now he wants to lick his shoe. But Caliban is not so drunk that he can't sense Trinculo's contempt. Trinculo can't believe that Caliban regards a fool like Stephano as a lord, and so he taunts him, "That a monster should be such a natural!" with still another pun. A "natural" is an idiot, but a monster, of course, is *un*natural. Stephano finally comes to Caliban's defense, and with his usual exaggeration he threatens to hang the jester.

Now Caliban is ready to inform Stephano of the scheme he's been formulating: he wants his new master to rid him of Prospero. As soon as he starts to outline his plot, however, Ariel enters and begins his mischief. When Caliban claims that Prospero cheated him out of the island, Ariel says, "Thou liest." Because the airy spirit is still invisible, Caliban and Stephano assume the words are Trinculo's. Stephano threatens to knock the jester's teeth out, and Trinculo, understandably, protests his innocence.

Caliban continues: once Stephano eliminates Prospero, the island will be Stephano's. His idea is to sneak up on Prospero and kill him while he's sleeping. Notice the parallel with Antonio and Sebastian's plot to murder Alonso in his sleep—another instance of symmetry in *The Tempest*. In some respects, the drunkards act out on a comic level what the noblemen attempt on a more serious plane.

When Ariel once again calls Caliban a liar, the monster turns on the innocent Trinculo and jeers him as a "pied ninny," referring to his multicolored jester's costume. He threatens to refuse to show Trinculo where to find fresh water on the island. Stephano's threat, to "make a stockfish out of" him, is more direct: stockfish was dried cod that had been beaten flat. Again, Trinculo claims he's blameless. But when Ariel repeats, for the third time, "Thou liest," Stephano grabs the jester and pummels him, to Caliban's delight. (Caliban's sadistic pleasure is another indication of his ignoble nature.) As you read, try to imagine this broad and basic comedy performed: if it's staged well it is hilarious.

Once Trinculo is beaten to Caliban's satisfaction, the monster continues with his scheme, offering a list of sadistic ways to kill Prospero. (He obviously enjoys picturing each one.) Stephano must remember to seize Prospero's magic books, because without them, Caliban claims, the magician can't command his spirits. At this point he also mentions the remarkably beautiful Miranda.

NOTE: You've probably observed that the monster continues to talk largely in verse while Stephano and Trinculo speak in prose. In fact, scholars have noticed that even Caliban's prose speeches seem to split into lines of poetry. These lines may well be "verse fossils" of an earlier draft of the play, but what this means isn't clear. Perhaps Shakespeare intended at first to have Caliban speak solely in verse, and then changed his mind. It's possible, too, that some other writer may have done some tampering. And there's always the chance—since the lines don't divide exactly—that their closeness to verse is just a coincidence.

When Caliban says, "I never saw a woman/But only Sycorax my dam and she" ("she" is Miranda), Shakespeare has drawn a further parallel between the monster and the young women, who's already said that she can't remember seeing any men other than her father and Ferdinand. Recall that in Act I, Scene II, Shakespeare offered a parallel, or at least a contrast, in the way Miranda and Caliban were educated. Whereas education had beneficial effects on Miranda's high nature, its effects on Caliban's low one were extremely harmful. Keep these parallels in mind, as they continue developing until the end of the play.

Stephano is charmed with the prospect of so beautiful a woman; thus, he drunkenly decides to follow Caliban's advice and kill Prospero. Then he'll rule the island with Miranda as his queen and Caliban and Trinculo as his court. Ariel eavesdrops on Stephano's plan and pledges to report the plot to Prospero. Stephano is so elated with the plan that he begins a "catch" (a musical round similar to "Row, row, row your boat"). He gets the tune wrong, however, and Ariel, playing pipe and drum, corrects him. This invisible music startles them all. Trinculo, sure that it comes from demons, cries out, "O, forgive me my sins!" Stephano is more defiant. But Caliban calms them both. In another unexpected contrast, he interrupts this farce to deliver one of the loveliest speeches in the play, in which he assures them that there's music all over the island, and that it's nothing to fear. Once again, there's something wonderful about the way in which music charms the monster.

NOTE: Music It should be apparent by now that music is a vital element in *The Tempest*. In fact, this relatively brief play has more songs in it that any of Shakespeare's others, as well as frequent intervals of instrumental music. While the songs don't always advance the plot, they seem perfectly designed to fit each singer. Thus, Ariel's music is light, airy, often mysterious; Caliban's is robust; Stephano's is coarse. And, as you can see from Caliban's speech, the instrumental music is a convenient stage device for making the island seem truly enchanted.

Caliban's speech does calm the two men. Stephano is pleased at the prospect of ruling an island where music is free. Trinculo, at first so fearful, now wants to pursue the music. They follow Ariel out, with Caliban in the lead, and Trinculo, still perhaps a little nervous, bringing up the rear.

ACT III, SCENE III

By now Alonso and his court are thoroughly exhausted from searching for Ferdinand. Gonzalo complains that the "forthrights and meanders"— the straight paths and winding ones—have fatigued him, and Alonso calls for a rest. Never an optimist, the King, after this long and fruitless search, has given up all hope of finding the Prince.

As the others rest, the conspirators confer. Sebastian assures Antonio that he's still ready to kill his brother. Antonio advises waiting until nighttime, since the men are so tired that they won't be able to maintain much of a guard.

An unusually elaborate stage direction calls for "Solemn and strange music," associated as usual with magic. Suddenly the spirits enter, bearing a banquet, and perform a highly courteous dance inviting the men to dine. When they depart they leave Prospero perched, unseen, at the top of the stage.

Naturally, the men are astounded. Sebastian calls the spectacle a "living drollery"—a puppet-show that's come to life. He and Antonio agree that from now on they'll believe all travelers' tales, no matter how preposterous they sound. Gonzalo is more impressed with the spirits' behavior: they may be "of monstrous shape" but their manners are so "gentle" and "kind" that they surpass those of most human beings. Prospero notes how right Gonzalo is, especially since some of the men in his own company are "worse than devils."

Alonso, too, is astonished; he observes that although the shapes didn't speak, they communicated an "excellent" message. Prospero, still unheard, utters the proverb, "Praise in departing," meaning that one should not praise the host until the meal is over. Soon Alonso will think the spirits' message is far less excellent.

Sebastian is hungry, but Alonso hesitates, apparently wary of a meal served by spirits. But the confident Gonzalo reassures him: after all, when they were boys, there were many wonders that they would never have believed in, but now every traveler knows that these wonders really exist. By extension, therefore, there's no need to fear what they've witnessed simply because it's unfamiliar.

NOTE: When Gonzalo mentions "Each putter-out of five for one," he's referring to an early form of insurance at a time when travel was quite dangerous. Travelers leaving England would deposit a sum of money with an agent. If they didn't come back, the agent kept the money; but if they returned safe, he paid it back fivefold. (Some scholars have argued that if Shakespeare was talking about travelers, he should have said "each putter-out of *one for five*.")

Alonso is convinced, partly because he's so grief-stricken over Ferdinand that he doesn't care whether or not the food harms him. He invites the others to join him. But just as they're starting to dine, thunder and lightning break out; Ariel, transformed into a harpy, swoops down and steals their food. Harpies are legendary creatures of Greek and Roman mythology. They have faces of women and the bodies of predatory birds and not only steal food, but leave a sickening stench behind them. This scene is based on events in Book III of Virgil's *Aeneid*, the great Roman epic poem. When Shakespeare's noblemen draw their swords against the harpies, they're following Virgil; as in Virgil, their attempt to kill them is useless. The stage direction mentions only Ariel, but some of his fellow spirits probably appeared as additional harpies, since Ariel refers to his "fellow ministers."

NOTE: Staging the banquet By the time *The Tempest* was written, stage machinery had grown quite sophisticated; the banquet scene, therefore, was probably produced as elaborately as anything Shakespeare ever wrote. The stage directions call for the banquet to vanish "with a quaint device." Although we don't know exactly how this was accomplished, one scholar conjectures that the table rose onto the stage through a trap door, a cloth around the sides concealing a stagehand underneath. Ariel descended from above and covered the table with his harpy's wings; meanwhile, the stagehand snatched the food through a trap door in the table. Thus, when Ariel removed his wings, the food was gone. Shakespeare may have placed Prospero "at the top"—above the upper stage—so the actor could give signals to the musicians behind him, who in turn would relay them to the stagehands. The scene, with music, thunder and lightning, and special effects, must have formed an impressive spectacle.

Ariel the harpy addresses a long speech to Alonso, Sebastian, and Antonio—"three men of sin." (Apparently the others don't hear it.) The spirit explains that the ever-hungry sea has put them on an uninhabited island because they're not fit to live among men. He claims he's made them insane, and hints that often, with the courage of that kind of madness, men kill themselves. At this point they draw their swords against him, but he taunts them that they can no more kill harpies than they could kill the sea by stabbing it. Besides, their swords have suddenly become too heavy for them. (Prospero's magic seems to be at work here.) Then he tells them the reason they're being punished: for usurping Prospero's dukedom and casting him and Miranda out to sea. (Note that this is the first you hear of Sebastian's involvement in the plot against Prospero.) The powers of destiny haven't forgotten the crime—they've only delayed the punishment. Now it has started, however, with the tempest and the loss of Ferdinand. Ariel promises the villains "Ling'ring perdition"—prolonged damnation, worse than any quick death—unless they repent their crime and lead a blameless life on the desolate island. With a clap of thunder, he vanishes. The other spirits reappear with "mocks and mows" (jeers and grimaces)—behavior very different from the elaborate courtesy which earlier led Gonzalo to praise their manners.

NOTE: Ariel has delivered the classic Christian message: Repent and be saved; repent or be damned. Shakespeare will further develop this deeply religious theme in the final act.

Prospero praises Ariel's excellent performance, noting that the other spirits have done well, too. He's pleased that his enemies "now are in my power" and he exits to visit Ferdinand and Miranda.

Gonzalo, meanwhile, is puzzled: why is Alonso suddenly staring so wildly? Alonso's answer seems almost deranged: the waves, the winds, the thunder spoke to him during the tempest, and what they uttered was: "Prospero." (When he says, "it did bass my tresspass," he's using a musical figure, turning his crime or "trespass" into music to which the thunder, speaking Prospero's name, provided the bass line.) Understanding that Ferdinand was snatched from him as a punishment, he determines in a fit of despair to kill himself and join his son in the underwater mud. Alonso then runs out.

Sebastian and Antonio, however, don't seem to feel the remorse that Ariel told them would be their only salvation. Instead, they agree to fight the spirits, even though they've just seen how useless that is. They too dash out.

The others may not have heard Ariel's speech, but Gonzalo at least understands what's happened: their old guilt about Prospero has worked on the "three men of sin" like a slow poison and suddenly driven them mad. Gonzalo suggests that they be watched closely lest they do harm to themselves in their insanity.

ACT IV

ACT IV, SCENE I

Lines 1–59

Prospero is addressing Ferdinand in a tone very different from his earlier crustiness. The trials he put the young man through were severe, but Miranda was worth the struggle. Prospero estimates her value at "a third of mine own life," a line that readers have interpreted in several ways. Is he dividing "mine own life" into himself, his dead wife, and Miranda; or, perhaps, into himself, Miranda, and his kingdom? Or does he mean that raising his fifteen-year-old daughter has taken a third of his forty-five years? In any case, he's offering her now to the young prince, who has passed all his tests to Prospero's great satisfaction. Ferdinand may be smiling at Prospero's extravagant praise, because Prospero assures him that he isn't exaggerating, but Ferdinand declares that he'd believe him even if an oracle pronounced the opposite. (An oracle, in Greek and Roman religion, was the utterance of a deity, usually spoken by a priest or priestess.)

Prospero then delivers a speech that has caused many readers to wonder about its meaning. There's nothing unusual in praising chastity before marriage—many parents still do it. But Prospero speaks so harshly—more like the severe old father of the earlier acts—that his words border on gracelessness. Instead of emphasizing chastity's positive aspects, he delivers a warning that is very nearly a threat: if Ferdinand takes Miranda's virginity before their wedding day, their marriage will be full of "disdain" and "discord"; he also speaks of "barren hate," implying that they won't have any children.

Some readers have felt that Prospero's tone is inappropriate here—hasn't he been hard enough on Ferdinand already? Do you agree with them? Ferdinand's reply, however, shows that he isn't offended. He agrees that premarital sex would threaten the peace of the marriage, as well as "fair issue" or healthy children. He promises Prospero that no matter what the temptation, he'll preserve Miranda's virginity so he'll be able to enjoy the "edge"—the keen pleasure—of sexual love on their wedding day. He ends by picturing that day,

> When I shall think or Phoebus' steeds are
>   foundered
> Or Night kept chained below.

That is, he'll be so impatient for his wedding night that it will seem either that the horses that draw the sun god, Phoebus, have gone lame, prolonging the daylight, or that Night (personified here) is being kept in chains so he can't arrive when he's supposed to. It's an elaborate flourish, not the kind of speech you would choose in the heat of passion. Ferdinand is thus talking about chastity abstractly.

NOTE: Chastity and self-control   Prospero's speech is more than the advice of a protective father to his prospective son-in-law; it's central to the meaning of *The Tempest*. Chastity is a convenient symbol for general self-control, an ability to govern one's appetites. The personification of appetite in the play is Caliban, who has no control over his own desires, and who, you'll remember, once tried to rape Miranda. Thus the contrast between him and the chaste Ferdinand is clear. In Shakespeare's day, self-control was regarded as an important attribute of the successful magician as well as the successful ruler. You could argue that Prospero's downfall in Milan was due to his lack of self-control: he allowed Antonio to take over the reins of government so he could satisfy his own uncontrollable appetite for knowledge. On his island, Prospero has to learn the lesson of self-control. You'll see him put this lesson into practice in the fifth act, when he must demonstrate his self-control by restraining his anger.

Prospero, pleased by Ferdinand's speech, leaves the young man chatting with Miranda while he calls Ariel, who appears immediately. The magician commends the way Ariel and the lesser spirits ("thy meaner fellows") carried off the performance at the banquet. Now he wants them to perform for Ferdinand and Miranda. He tells Ariel to bring the lesser spirits (the "rabble") and gives him command over them. Ariel declares his readiness with a light and airy five-line rhyme.

When Prospero turns around again, evidently the young lovers are doing more than chatting, because Prospero has to admonish them to be more temperate. Probably they are embracing. Oaths, after all, mean very little in the heat of the moment. Ferdinand's response has been variously interpreted:

> The white cold virgin snow upon my heart
> Abates the ardor of my liver.

The liver was considered the seat of sexual passion. Some readers think Ferdinand is saying that the idea of Miranda, like snow on his heart, cools his passion. Other readers, however, think he's speaking more literally: Miranda's breast against his heart cools his passion—though it's hard to imagine, no matter how pure Miranda is, how embracing her could lessen his passion. Of course, a young man who has been caught like Ferdinand has, might have to talk his way rapidly out of an embarrassing situation.

Prospero replies with a curt "Well," but it's uncertain whether he accepts Ferdinand's response or just doesn't want to argue. He summons Ariel and his fellow spirits to start the masque.

NOTE: "No tongue! All eyes! Be silent." Prospero's admonition is more than just a request for polite attention. It was thought that silence was absolutely necessary during magical operations; the spirits would flee at the sound of human voices (which in fact is very like what happens at the close of the masque). Later Prospero warns, "Hush and be mute,/Or else our spell is marred."

Lines 60–142
Before considering the play-within-a-play that the spirits now present in Ferdinand and Miranda's honor, you will need some background on this unique form of drama, known as a masque. The masque evolved from older spectacles and games; in its medieval form, it involved a surprise visit by masked dancers to an unwitting person's home.

By the time of Queen Elizabeth I, who ruled England from 1558 until her death in 1603, it had become popular at court and had already developed formal conventions. But it was really under Elizabeth's successor, James I, who ruled from 1603 to 1625, that the masque reached its height as a dramatic form.

The story line of a masque was often insignificant; the emphasis was on spectacle. Huge sums of money were spent on sets and costumes. Music and dance were also important elements. It's generally agreed that nothing more spectacular has ever been presented on the English stage. You might even compare these spectacles to multimillion-dollar science-fiction films, especially because these movies also usually depend more on spectacle than on content.

Masques were often performed on such special occasions as a wedding or, as here, a betrothal. This betrothal masque made *The Tempest* a particularly appropriate play to revive at court, as indeed it was, during the winter of 1612–1613, as part of a series of entertainments that celebrated the betrothal of King James' daughter Elizabeth to the Elector Palatine (an elector was a German prince) during his visit to the English court.

Because the masque was such a popular form, it's not surprising that several of Shakespeare's plays show its influence. In addition to the actual masque in *The Tempest*, some readers have pointed out masquelike elements in the overall structure of the play. Prospero resembles a traditional masque "presenter," a ringmaster who introduces the other characters and controls their actions. In a sense, the action of *The Tempest* has as much in common with the static spectacle of the masque as with the developing tension and resolution of the traditional five-act drama. Little true tension develops; there's never much uncertainty about the outcome of the plot. This isn't to say that *The Tempest* is a masque in disguise; however, you can see that Shakespeare responded to one of the popular dramatic forms of his time.

The masque opens with a speech by Iris, who in Greek mythology was the messenger of the gods as well as goddess of the rainbow. Thus, Ceres addresses her as "many-colored messenger" and as "heavenly bow." Iris is speaking for Juno, queen of the gods. (Ceres and Juno are Roman names for the Greek goddesses Demeter and Hera.) Although her meaning is quite simple ("Please come"), Shakespeare gives her sixteen lines of highly elaborate, highly artificial verse. The diction in this masque is far more stilted than anywhere else in *The Tempest*, which has led some readers to suspect that another writer had a hand in it. In fact, however, the conventions of the masque demanded a much more formal diction than did a five-act drama. In addition, there's probably an element of parody: Shakespeare may be poking gentle fun at the stilted verse of the popular masques. Shakespeare's "plays within plays" are often cast in verse much more artificial than his usual expert poetry. You may be familiar with the rhymed couplets of the traveling players in Act III of *Hamlet*, or the ridiculous "Pyramus and Thisby" in Act V of *A Midsummer Night's Dream*.

As goddess of the harvest and, by extension, of fertility, Ceres is a natural choice to bless a young couple who want to have children. In a similar vein, Juno is the protector of marriage. Iris's speech includes numerous images of the fertility associated with her: fields of wheat, rye, barley, pruned vineyards, and so forth. Iris announces that Juno is already approaching in a chariot drawn by the peacocks that were her special birds. Although the stage direction says, "Juno descends," Juno doesn't speak for another thirty lines. It's possible that she appeared at this point in a device that descended very slowly to the stage.

Ceres enters, with an equally elaborate speech and an equally simple point: What does Juno want? Iris replies, more briefly, that Juno wants her to celebrate and bless a betrothal, "a contract of true love."

Ceres returns to the theme of chastity that Prospero and Ferdinand discussed earlier. She wants to know if Venus and her son Cupid are with Juno. Although Juno is the protector of marriage, Venus is the goddess of love and of the passion about which Prospero has been warning Ferdinand. Cupid carried a bow and arrows, and anyone he pierced would fall passionately in love.

Ceres has a particular reason to resent Venus and Cupid, who she says "did plot/The means that dusky Dis my daughter got." She's alluding to the way the god of the underworld, Dis (better known as Hades or Pluto), kidnapped her daughter Persephone (Proserpine). Ceres' grief was said to be the cause of winter.

In a reply rich with classical allusions, Iris assures Ceres that although Venus and Cupid had been planning some mischief, it's been averted. Iris may be referring to the embrace between Ferdinand and Miranda that Prospero promptly ended. The dove is Venus's bird; thus, she and Cupid travel "Dove-drawn" away from them and toward Paphos, the city in Cyprus that was the center of her cult. She is referred to as "Mars's hot minion" because Mars, the god of war, was her lover. The core of Iris's speech is her assurance "that no bed-right shall be paid/Till Hymen's torch be lighted." Hymen is the god of the wedding feast; he was often pictured carrying a torch. Iris means that Ferdinand and Miranda won't sleep together until after the wedding.

Finally Juno appears, greets Ceres, and invites her to join her in singing a blessing to Ferdinand and Miranda. Their song was probably divided, with Juno singing the first four lines, which refer specifically to her, and Ceres singing the remaining eight, which are mainly about her particular concerns, harvest and abundance ("foison"). When she sings,

> Spring come to you at the farthest
> In the very end of harvest

she's saying, "May spring come right on the heels of fall"; in other words, "May your lives be without winter." The sentiment was a conventional one in Shakespeare's day.

Ferdinand is so impressed with the masque that he can't resist offering a compliment. He asks whether the players are spirits; Prospero confirms that they are and that he called them up himself. Ferdinand chatters on that Prospero is wise and that the island resembles paradise. At this point, Prospero warns him to be quiet: the masque isn't finished, and human talk could break the spell.

At the behest of Juno and Ceres, Iris calls forth a group of Naiads, or water nymphs, and another group of reapers. The masque closes with its traditional ending, a dance. (In court masques, the dancers were often drawn from among the spectators.) Toward the end of this graceful entertainment, however, Prospero suddenly remembers the conspiracy of Caliban, Trinculo, and Stephano to murder him. His face darkens, and his agitated words break the spell. Sorrowfully, the spirits vanish in a confused mass.

Lines 143–266

It's probably at this point that Prospero seems least godlike, most human and fallible. The change that's come over him is so sudden, and so extreme, that it upsets both Ferdinand and Miranda. Miranda says she's never seen her father so angry. But Prospero notices their concern and urges them not to worry. Then, beginning with "Our revels now are ended," he delivers the most famous and, many readers believe, the most beautiful lines of poetry in the play.

The masque, by its very nature, was a form that left the audience thinking about the transitory nature of life. Its time span was brief, and at its end the audience was probably thinking rather sadly about how the maskers would disband and the breathtaking scenery would be dismantled. ("The cloud-capped towers, the gorgeous palaces,/The solemn temples, The great globe itself" were probably all pieces of masque scenery.) Thus, the kind of sentiment that Prospero now delivers was, not surprisingly, rather commonplace at the end of masques. After viewing a vision of perfection—an

ideal world of beauty and abundance, a world
without winter—the thought of Caliban returns
Prospero sharply to the real world of brutality and
evil. His immediate anger yields to profound
depression. As he contemplates the end of the
masque, it seems to him for a moment that life is
equally insubstantial: "We are such stuff/As dreams
are made on [of]." Have you ever felt this way in
a moment of depression—you can work, study,
exhaust yourself trying to do good; however, the
final reality is death. As Prospero says, "our little
life/Is rounded"—that is, finished off—"with a
sleep."

But Prospero at least recognizes that his bleak
thoughts are the result of his melancholy mood.
He tells the young lovers to bear with him: he only
needs to walk it off and collect himself. They understand and exit obediently, wishing him peace
of mind.

Prospero   summons   Ariel: "Come   with   a
thought." Traditionally, spirits were supposed to
be able to travel as fast as thought, and thus appear at their masters' desire. Prospero reminds him
that it's time to deal with Caliban, and Ariel tells
him that the matter was on his mind, too, "when
I presented Ceres."

NOTE: This phrase could mean simply that Ariel
was the "presenter" of the masque, but it might
also mean "when I played Ceres." Ariel probably
played one of the roles, though Iris would be as
likely a choice as Ceres.

At a question from Prospero, Ariel tells you

what's happened to Caliban and his cohorts since you last saw them. They were drunk when he surprised them with his magic music. They followed, unable to resist, like calves after their mother. Then Ariel started playing tricks. He led them through briars and thorns, and finally into a pond with a coat of filthy scum. There they stood, with the water chin-high and smelling so awful that it "O'erstunk their feet."

Prospero is rather vindictively satisfied at this report, and he sends Ariel off for "stale"—decoys—with which to trap the conspirators. He then utters some extremely bitter thoughts on the subject of Caliban. The monster, he says, is "a born devil," which is probably literally true, as Caliban's father was a demon.

NOTE: Don't forget that the "three men of sin" (Alonso, Antonio, and Sebastian) are, according to Prospero, "worse than devils." The difference between Caliban and them lies in their respective low and high natures. Caliban was born low; thus, he's not responsible for his beastliness. This is not the case with the noblemen, however.

Prospero assails Caliban as a beast "on whose nature/Nurture can never stick." This pun summarizes one of the play's important themes. Low-born Caliban has a low nature; thus, "nurture"—Prospero's nurturing education—can't stick to it and do him any good. The embittered Prospero laments the humane efforts he wasted on the monster: "all, all lost, quite lost." In that aching repetition, you can sense Prospero's anguish. But perhaps Prospero is really lamenting his own failure. After all, it isn't Caliban's fault that he can't be educated, but it may be Prospero's fault that he failed to recognize this fact. Prospero has failed twice to keep persons or beasts at their proper station. First he elevated Antonio to the level of ruler while he himself studied undisturbed; then he tried to educate Caliban. In both cases it may be impossible for Prospero to reverse the damage. Antonio hasn't shown any signs of repenting. And there's no way for Prospero to take back Caliban's education and return his contentment with his low station.

Instead of accepting the blame, Prospero seems to vent a rather cruel bitterness: "I will plague them all,/Even to roaring." Do you think he is being unfair? He may have been mistaken in trying to educate Caliban, but he was erring on the side of kindness. Surely he has the right to be angry upon discovering a plot to murder him. Or do you feel that as a ruler, Prospero should have known better than to treat Caliban as he did? To what extent do you think Prospero is wrong?

NOTE: Prospero observes, "And as with age his body uglier grows,/So his mind cankers"—his thoughts grow more evil. Note again that physical ugliness is related to moral vice, a theme discussed in the Note at the end of Act I, Scene II.

Ariel returns laden with "glistering apparel," perhaps the "rich garments" that Gonzalo long ago supplied Prospero with. When the three conspirators enter, they are soaking wet and smell terrible. Stephano and Trinculo are particularly irked that they've lost their bottles; Stephano is ready to dive for the wine. Caliban pleads for quiet: he doesn't want them to wake Prospero. Then Stephano and Trinculo notice the garments.

NOTE: Trinculo's exclamation—"O King Stephano! O peer! O worthy Stephano, look what a wardrobe here is for thee"—is a joking allusion to a popular ballad. One version of it is sung in Act II, Scene III of Shakespeare's *Othello:*

> King Stephen was and a worthy peer
> His breeches cost him but a crown.

Stephano and Trinculo grab the clothes so greedily that they forget all about their murder plot. Caliban is more level-headed. He warns them to ignore the trousers, which are a decoy, but they act like children, their appetites uncontrolled, enthralled by every new bauble. They pile fine clothes on the protesting monster.

NOTE: Puns on "line" Prospero directs Ariel to hang the garments on a line. It's uncertain whether the words means "clothes-line" or "lime tree," but it doesn't really matter. Stephano and Trinculo, however, offer a number of puns on the word "line." First it's the "line" on which the clothes are hanging. Next a jerkin (jacket) is "under the line"—across the equator. (It's a "bald jerkin," apparently, because when people crossed the equator, they supposedly ran fevers that made their hair fall out.) Then they're stealing "by line and level"—literally, by plumb-line and carpenter's level, but the phrase means "according to rule." When Trinculo tells Caliban to put some lime on his fingers, he's probably taking the pun even further. "Lime" is birdlime, a sticky substance that was used to snare birds, and which was almost a synonym for theft (similar to "sticky fingers").

Finally, justice arrives, in the form of further spectacle. The spirits return as hounds, set on by Prospero and Ariel, and chase away the three conspirators. You can imagine the comic possibilities. But perhaps there's an undertone of cruelty, too, as Prospero orders his goblins to torment them with convulsions, cramps, and pinches. Ariel cries, "Hark, they roar!"—fulfiling Prospero's vow to "plague them all,/Even to roaring." This is Prospero's supreme moment of power: "At this hour/ Lies at my mercy all mine enemies." As the act closes, he's in complete control.

ACT V

ACT V, SCENE I

Lines 1–57

As previously noted, *The Tempest* is one of the few plays that Shakespeare actually cast in classical five-act structure. Hence the break between Acts IV and V, even though Act V opens with the same two characters onstage and little, if any, time having past.

It's six o'clock, the hour that Prospero earlier forecast would mark the end of his plan. The "three men of sin," Ariel informs him, are gathered in a nearby lime ("line") grove, gripped by an enchanted madness from which only Prospero can release them. The others are mourning them, with the tearful Gonzalo forming an especially pitiful spectacle. The sight would make Prospero's feelings grow tender, Ariel tells him; his own feelings certainly would if he were human. Remember that Ariel is a spirit; thus, he can only imagine human feelings.

Some readers view Ariel's comment as the turning point in the drama, because it prompts Prospero's forgiveness. Others argue that because Prospero has arranged the marriage of Ferdinand and Miranda, he was obviously planning to forgive his enemies all along. Which view do you agree with? Prospero won't be outdone by a spirit when he himself is "One of their kind"—that is, human—and thus should be "kindlier" affected than the inhuman Ariel. (This pun on "kind"— both "kindhearted" and "sort,"—is one of Shakespeare's favorites.) Prospero doesn't downplay his sufferings. He's still aggrieved when he thinks of his enemies and "their high wrongs." It's something of a higher order than emotion—"my nobler reason" working " 'gainst my fury"—that convinces him to forgive them. He forgives them not so much because he wants to as because he ought to: "the rarer action is/In virtue than in vengeance." This concise observation crystallizes a major theme of the play. Christian virtue, with its great emphasis on forgiveness, is a higher mode of behavior than pagan revenge. Remember that this sentiment, though conventional, was uttered before an audience for whom the revenge tragedy was a major form of entertainment.

NOTE: The Religious interpretation   Do you see *The Tempest* as a deeply Christian drama? If so, you will place a great deal of emphasis on the above lines, as well as on the ones that follow. Prospero declares that his only purpose in tormenting Alonso, Sebastian, and Antonio is to make them repent. As you'll recall, this was also Ariel's message in Act III, Scene III. Readers who support a religious interpretation point out that Prospero isn't merely godlike: he stands in relation to the other characters much as God traditionally does to humanity—judging, punishing, forgiving. In the figure of Ariel you might think he even has an angel. Other readers, however, feel that this interpretation can be carried too far. They point out that Prospero, powerful and wise as he is, isn't perfect. You already know of his failures with Antonio and Caliban. In addition, his forgiveness, though noble, is tinged with anger; it isn't quite the all-embracing love of a completely merciful God.

At a word from Prospero, Ariel leaves to fetch the wrongdoers. Prospero now delivers the soliloquy that's generally known as his farewell to his art. This speech can be divided into three roughly equal parts. The first eight lines form an address to his magical helpers: the fairies who leave no footprints on the beach, the puppet-sized elves who make small circles of discolored grass, sometimes called "fairy circles," on the ground, and who make mushrooms grow overnight (a natural phenomenon that seems magical), and so forth.

Lines 41 to 50 describe some of Prospero's magical feats. He's dimmed the sun at noon. He's made the wind blow and created huge waves (which he describes as setting the sea at war with the sky). He's called forth thunder and lightning and shaken the ground—in other words, he's created tempests. He's even summoned the dead from their graves.

NOTE: Prospero's magic   Prospero is clearly a good magician whose "white magic" is very different from the "black magic" of Caliban's mother, the witch Sycorax. White magicians gained their abilities only through long study and strict self-control; black magicians made pacts with demons. (Sycorax worshipped the demon Setebos and mated with a devil to produce Caliban.) Magic was a serious subject to Shakespeare's audience. King James I was an authority on the subject, and Shakespeare had to present magic very carefully on the stage. He could have created serious legal problems for himself and the King's Men if his play seemed to glorify black magic.

Prospero's list of his accomplishments has therefore created a snag for Shakespeare scholars. Getting spirits to work for them was the natural province of white magicians; however, raising storms, and especially raising the dead, were the domain of black magicians. Many of Prospero's claims seem to be based on lines in Book III of the *Metamorphoses* by the Roman poet Ovid. Shakespeare was apparently more engrossed in creating a play than in keeping the domains of white and black magicians separate. Raising the dead, which is found in the *Metamorphoses*, doesn't play a serious role in the plot. Raising a storm, however, does—it's essential both to the story and to the title of the play.

In any case, Prospero and Ariel's tempest doesn't harm anybody. It doesn't even stain the clothes of the survivors of the shipwreck. In fact, the storm that seemed so terrible will turn out to be a blessing. Thus, Prospero can hardly be convicted of performing evil magic. Nevertheless, the fact that Prospero now renounces his magic probably is related to the poor reputation sorcery had in Shakespeare's England. Prospero has accomplished his goals with his magic. Now he demonstrates his good faith by giving it up.

The last eight lines of Prospero's soliloquy comprise his actual renunciation. His plan completed, he says, he'll break and bury his magic staff and throw his magic book into the sea. But he'll require two or three more spells. The first is a "heavenly music" to bring Alonso, Antonio, and Sebastian out of their madness; a stage direction now calls for "solemn music."

NOTE: The autobiographical interpretation As was noted earlier, one popular theory identifies Prospero with Shakespeare himself. Like a skilled dramatic poet, Prospero manipulates the characters, involving them in situations that he created for them. In this interpretation, Prospero's magic stands for Shakespeare's poetry. Ariel and Caliban can even be regarded as two different aspects of the poet. Ariel, with his lightness, elegance, and speed-of-thought grace, is the poet's genius. Caliban is his appetite or desire, and the fact that Prospero keeps him chained down in a rocky den denotes the poet's self-control or self-discipline.

Prospero's farewell to his art is central to the autobiographical interpretation. *The Tempest* may be the last play that Shakespeare wrote, or wrote alone. Just before or, more probably, just after he created it, he retired from theatrical life in London to the quiet country village of his birth, Stratford-on-Avon. We don't know why; he doesn't seem to have been ill. In his late forties, he could reflect on an active and successful career in the theater. Perhaps he just wanted to enjoy his leisure. In any case, readers looking for hints of autobiography see Prospero's farewell to his art as a parallel to Shakespeare's farewell to his own dramatic art. Indeed, there's something melancholy and final about the tone of the entire play.

On the other hand, some readers find the autobiographical interpretation unlikely. They argue that it isn't necessary to look outside the work to find its meaning. They feel that it's ludicrous to try to make *The Tempest* fit the mold of Shakespeare's life, about which very little is known. No matter how you feel about this interpretation, it's probably true that at this point in his own career,

Shakespeare could appreciate Prospero's emotions. It's this deep empathy that makes the speech so convincing.

Lines 58–215

Prospero has drawn a magic circle on the ground (a typical feature of magic ceremonies), into which Ariel leads Alonso and his court. All six men stand there frozen in enchantment, as the solemn melody gradually soothes the three maddened "men of sin." (Music was—and still is—a widely accepted therapy for nervous agitation.)

Although moved by Gonzalo's tears, Prospero can't resist rehashing the crimes committed against him. It's clear that though he's planning to forgive them, he still feels wronged. Because the men are regaining consciousness little by little, he sends Ariel to fetch the royal robes by which they'll recognize him as the deposed Duke of Milan.

As Ariel dresses Prospero, he sings the last of his fairy songs; this one tells of sucking nectar with the bees and riding on the backs of bats. Then Prospero sends him to the ship to get the master (captain) and the boatswain.

By now the noblemen are coming out of the spell. Gonzalo, the first to speak, calls on "some heavenly power" to get them off this eerie island. Note that even when he's terrified he trusts in Providence. Observing rank, Prospero speaks first to the flabbergasted king. He announces that he's the "wronged Duke of Milan," and before Alonso can respond he embraces him to demonstrate his lack of anger.

Alonso has endured so much in the past hours

that he doesn't know whether to believe Prospero
or not. At least Prospero feels real to the touch—
real enough to make Alonso grow defensive: "Thy
dukedom I resign," he quickly assures him. Of
course, Alonso has never been ruler of Prospero's
dukedom. He refers to the annual tribute that
Milan has been paying Naples since Prospero was
ousted.

Prospero embraces his old friend Gonzalo, who,
like Alonso, isn't quite sure that all this is really
happening. He's tasting "some subtleties o' th' isle,"
Prospero tells him. "Subtleties" were Renaissance
pastries in the shapes of castles, temples, and so
forth; Prospero is joking that Gonzalo can't believe
that what he's seeing is any more real than those
pastries.

Prospero welcomes them all; then, almost in the
same breath, he threatens Sebastian and Antonio.
He tells them in an aside that he knows all about
their plot against Alonso. With distinct overtones
of blackmail, perhaps in order to be able to keep
them in line in the future, he promises to remain
silent, at least for the moment.

NOTE: When Sebastian says, "The devil speaks
in him," he isn't merely making a rude comment.
Sebastian doesn't know that Prospero is a white
magician; thus, he has every reason to believe he's
a sorcerer in league with the devil.

Prospero now formally forgives Antonio. Read
this speech carefully; do you think Prospero has
conquered his anger and resentment? Notice that

he begins by addressing his brother formally, as "you"; however, with forgiveness comes the more intimate "thou" form:

> For you, most wicked sir, whom to call brother
> Would even infect my mouth, I do forgive
> Thy rankest fault—all of them; and require
> My dukedom of thee, which perforce I know
> Thou must restore.

NOTE: Forgiveness and repentance   This is one of several places in Shakespeare's comedies where a villain is forgiven even though he seems to deserve punishment rather than mercy. Some readers think Shakespeare is suggesting that humanity is so depraved that Prospero must forgive, because he can't spend his life drowning in hate. In a Christian view, everyone is flawed; everyone needs to be forgiven. Prospero knows how villainous Antonio is, but as he's explained already, he's using his reason instead of his anger because he knows that virtue is superior to vengeance.

It's not difficult for Prospero to forgive Alonso. The King is genuinely remorseful; he even pleads for forgiveness. In contrast, Antonio shows no remorse at all. Although both Ariel and Prospero have stressed the importance of repentance, Antonio gives no indication, either now or later, that he's sorry for his crimes. Prospero's kindness to him, like his kindness to Caliban, doesn't improve him, for Antonio is a true villain.

This doesn't mean, however, that Prospero is wrong to forgive Antonio. Shakespeare's audience was composed of Christians, and they would have agreed wholeheartedly that forgiveness was essential. It does mean that in the future, Prospero would be foolish to put much trust in his brother. As a wise prince, he should know how to temper Christian virtue with princely authority. In fact, he does this here, demonstrating virtue by forgiving, and authority by demanding the return of his dukedom.

As the thought of Ferdinand strikes Alonso again, he grows miserable once more. His loss is so deep, he claims, that patience can't help. Prospero gently rebukes him: You haven't really sought help from patience.

NOTE: Patience   This theme correlates with the notion of Providence. A good Christian trusts in God; no matter how terrible events seem on the surface, a benevolent God is watching. Gonzalo personifies this virtue. He's always hopeful, always optimistic; in contrast, impatient King Alonso is always sure that things will turn out for the worst. Thus, the tempest can teach Alonso an important lesson in patience: an apparent disaster can turn out to be a blessing.

Prospero claims that just as Alonso lost a son in the tempest, he, Prospero, lost a daughter. Prospero is referring to the fact that he has "lost" Miranda to Ferdinand. When Alonso cries out that he wishes their children were alive as King and Queen of Naples, Shakespeare is sharing a joke with you, because you know that not only are they alive, they *will* someday rule Naples.

Prospero promises to explain the whole story when there's more time. He welcomes them all again, and, he stretches the truth by claiming that here in his small dominion he has no subjects. But because Alonso has returned his dukedom, Prospero will give him "as good a thing." Probably by throwing back a curtain, he reveals Ferdinand and Miranda playing chess. The lovers, absorbed in their game, don't notice the others at first. Their words here have caused some confusion, but the general meaning is clear: Miranda is teasing Ferdinand about cheating, and he's swearing innocence.

Alonso's first response is characteristic: he's worried. If this is another illusion, he says pessimistically, then he'll have lost his son twice. Ferdinand notices his father, and his words express the theme of Providence in a nutshell: "Though the seas threaten, they are merciful."

Miranda's wonder is different. She's never seen so many people before, and she's awed by their noble appearance:

> How beauteous mankind is! O brave new world
> That has such people in't!

"Brave" is used here, as elsewhere, to mean excellent or fine.

These are among the most famous lines in *The Tempest*. The English novelist Aldous Huxley took the title of his futuristic novel *Brave New World* from them. He used the word ironically, though, because the future he depicted was anything but excellent. You can feel Miranda's wonder and admiration, and once more you should recall the notion of humanity created in God's image. But Shakespeare also knows that among these "goodly creatures" there lurk villains like Sebastian and Antonio. Thus, he gives Prospero the rather wry comment, " 'Tis new to thee." Prospero knows that the novelty will wear off; someday a sadder but wiser Miranda will learn to be more discriminating.

Like Ferdinand when he first beheld Miranda in Act I, Alonso is ready to take the young woman for a goddess. But Ferdinand, invoking Providence once again, assures him that she's mortal and she's his. He asks his father's pardon for having become betrothed without his permission. Alonso, in turn, wants to ask Miranda's pardon for his long-ago treachery in casting her and her father out to sea. Prospero, however, generously insists that there's no reason to dwell on an old sorrow.

Gonzalo hasn't said much up to this point. He explains that he was inwardly weeping, but now the good-natured old councilor is ready to talk. He calls upon the gods (a Renaissance convention; he means God) to bless the young couple. He sees clearly now that it was Providence that brought them to the island and turned disaster into blessing. And he asks,

> Was Milan thrust from Milan that his issue
> Should become kings of Naples?

That is, was the Duke of Milan, Prospero, banished from the city-state of Milan so that his offspring—Miranda's children and grandchildren—should become kings of Naples? After urging everyone to rejoice, he delivers the play's great message of Providence. In one voyage, Claribel found a husband at Tunis; Ferdinand found a wife "Where he himself was lost," on Prospero's island; and Prospero regained his dukedom. Perhaps he's overwhelmed by his beautiful language, because he adds that "all of us [found] ourselves/When no man was his own," suggesting that everyone has acquired self-knowledge. In the glory of the moment, no one thinks about what Gonzalo has said. It's true for Alonso and Ferdinand, but is it true for Sebastian, Antonio, and Gonzalo?

Alonso blesses the young lovers, and Gonzalo offers a hearty "Amen." Ariel returns leading the master of the ship and the boatswain, though they, of course, can't see him. You may be a little puzzled at Gonzalo's jokes about the boatswain's blasphemy, because there's nothing in the boatswain's lines either here or in Act I that really qualifies as blasphemy. Possibly the boatswain's oaths were censored from the published version of the play.

The boatswain tells an amazing story. He and the master were asleep with the other sailors (Ariel's enchanted sleep) and were wakened by horrible noises. Suddenly they were looking at the ship, which appeared to be in excellent condition, even though they'd given it up for ruined some three hours earlier. Then just as suddenly they were brought dazed to this spot.

Prospero, after promising to explain everything later, commands Ariel to bring in Caliban, Stephano, and Trinculo. They enter in their stolen clothing, and the tone shifts to comedy again.

NOTE: Caliban, Miranda, and human beauty
When Caliban regards the assembled group, he

cries, "These be brave spirits indeed!" This isn't the first time a character mistakes human beauty for a supernatural quality. Recall that in Act I, when Miranda and Ferdinand first saw each other, she thought he was a spirit or a "thing divine"; he addressed her as a goddess, just as Alonso did earlier in this act. Now Caliban, too, is sufficiently awed by human splendor to take the company for spirits. He immediately recognizes their superiority over him, just as he recognizes Prospero's authority: "How fine my master is!"—dressed in his robes as Duke of Milan. "I am afraid/He will chastise me." The implication is that the unteachable Caliban has learned a lesson; at least, he appears in a better light throughout this scene than do the unrepentant Sebastian and Antonio.

There is no mistaking the echo in Caliban's words of Miranda's "O brave new world/That has such people in't!" For the last time, Shakespeare draws a parallel between them; this time, however, rather than holding Caliban up for disapproval, Shakespeare compares him favorably with Miranda. In your last view of Caliban, you see a monster who's not entirely unsympathetic. If his nature is low, at least he's learned his place; unlike some of the higher-natured human beings on stage, at least he regrets his wrongs.

When Antonio sees Caliban, his reaction is very much like Stephano's and Trinculo's in Act II. He calls the monster a "fish" (a reference to Caliban's general oddity, not to his aquatic nature) and reflects that he's "marketable," that is, that he could be displayed as a freak.

Prospero reveals that Stephano, Trinculo, and Caliban robbed him and plotted to kill him. But he doesn't mention Antonio and Sebastian's plot against Alonso. Stephano and Trinculo, he declares, are Alonso's men; he acknowledges Caliban as his own.

NOTE: This straightforward statement has been cited by readers who support an autobiographical reading of the play. These readers think that Prospero is saying that this dark, physical, greedy thing (Caliban) is one side of his personality, but he keeps it under control. Do you agree, or do you have another explanation?

Trinculo lightens the mood by making puns on "in a pickle" (in a mess) and "pickled" (both drunk and preserved). He adds that he's so pickled that he won't have to worry about flies, for pickling preserved meat from flies. Stephano is in so much pain from the briars, the pond, and the goblin hounds Prospero and Ariel set on them that he says he's "not Stephano, but a cramp."

But Prospero's forgiving mood is pervasive, and he sends Caliban off, with Stephano and Trinculo, to clean his cell, promising a pardon if Caliban does his task well. Caliban's reply tells you that he may really have learned something from his experiences. He may be one of the characters who, as Gonzalo suggested, has acquired self-knowledge. He resolves to "be wise hereafter,/And seek for grace"; he perceives what a fool he was to mistake Stephano and Trinculo for gods. Standing next to the rest of the magnificent company, he probably sees them more easily for what they really are.

Alonso orders Stephano and Trinculo to put the treasure back where they found it, and Sebastian adds, "Or stole it rather." Both Alonso and Sebastian helped steal Milan from Prospero; Sebastian even plotted to steal the crown from Alonso. Do you find their lines here hypocritical? Shakespeare may be making gentle fun of them here, but he doesn't press the point.

Prospero tells the group that he'll relate the story of his life on the island. After that, he promises, they'll sail back to Naples, where Ferdinand and Miranda will be married; then he'll return to Milan, where "Every third thought shall be my grave." In Act IV he'd said that Miranda made up "a third of mine own life,/Or that for which I live." Perhaps every first and second thought will be of his daughter and his dukedom. Or it may be a figure of speech for thinking a great deal about death.

Prospero's last promise is that the winds will be so helpful that their ship will catch up with the rest of King Alonso's fleet before it reaches Naples. Speeding the ship homeward is Ariel's last assignment; after that, he tells the spirit, "Be free, and fare thou well!" With this command, the curtain falls on the final act.

Epilogue

At the end of Act V, the actor playing Prospero returns to the stage and addresses the audience directly in twenty brief, rhyming lines. He requests that just as he pardoned Antonio, the audience should pardon any faults in the production.

Prospero's words here continue to stress the theme of forgiveness, but his appeal for approval and, specifically, applause ("the help of your good hands") was a conventional way to end a comedy.

A STEP BEYOND

Tests and Answers

TESTS

Test 1

1. During the tempest of the first scene, _____
   Gonzalo finds reason for hope because the
   boatswain has the type of face
   A. that's headed for the gallows, not
      drowning
   B. that won't give up
   C. that's blessed by divine providence

2. Prospero's attempt to educate Caliban fails _____
   because Caliban
   A. has a nature that's too low to benefit
      from education
   B. will never forgive him for taking over
      the island
   C. has already learned too many spells
      from his mother, the witch Sycorax

3. Many of the characters in *The Tempest* are _____
   paired, but one of the following is *not* a
   pair:
   A. Ariel and Caliban
   B. Antonio and Alonso
   C. Miranda and Ferdinand

4. Gonzalo and Alonso represent the voices _____
   of

A. patience and impatience
B. servitude and authority
C. age and youth

5. Trinculo, Stephano, and Antonio all have   _____
the same reaction to Caliban:
A. he's too ugly to be trusted
B. he ought to be freed
C. he could bring a profit if he were
displayed as a freak

6. Ferdinand and Miranda's love helps heal   _____
the rift between Prospero and
A. Caliban   B. Alonso   C. Antonio

7. In his speech to the "three men of sin,"   _____
Ariel tells them that
  I. he's made them insane
 II. they're at the mercy of Prospero
III. their only hope is to repent and lead
    a good life
A. I and II only   B. II and III only
C. I and III only

8. The language of the spirits' masque in Act   _____
IV is different from that of the rest of the
play in that
A. it's much richer in metaphors
B. it uses the special grammar peculiar to
masques
C. it's more elaborate and artificial

9. Prospero's decision to forgive his enemies   _____
is apparently prompted by
A. Miranda's plea that he be merciful to
Ferdinand's father

   B. Ariel's comment that he would feel
      sorry for them if he were human
   C. his guilt about the torment he's put
      them through

10. The character who shows no remorse for _____
his wrongs is
   A. Caliban   B. Alonso   C. Antonio

11. What is your final judgment of Prospero? Analyze
his character carefully, considering his bad points
as well as his good ones.

12. Consider the role of physical beauty in the play.

13. Discuss the parallels among the various schemes in
the play, and the reasons for these parallels.

14. Compare and contrast Ariel and Caliban.

15. Analyze Gonzalo's character, and explain the old
councilor's function in the play.

Test 2

1. Prospero's mistakes as Duke of Milan _____
included
   I. granting Antonio too much power
  II. having too little patience to trust
     divine providence
 III. studying too much and governing too
     little
   A. I and II only   B. II and III only
   C. I and III only

2. To say that Shakespeare observes the _____
classical unities in *The Tempest* means that
   A. the play is based on the Greek and
      Roman classics

B. the poetic diction is unified with the action
C. everything happens in the same place and on the same day

3. Prospero treats Ferdinand harshly because _____
   A. he's the son of his old enemy Alonso
   B. he doesn't feel Miranda is ready to marry
   C. he wants to test the young man's worth

4. Antonio and Sebastian's plot against Alonso _____
   parallels
   A. Prospero and Ariel's plot against Alonso
   B. the original plot against Prospero
   C. Stephano and Trinculo's plot to save the wine

5. Caliban mistakes Stephano and Trinculo for _____
   A. traders   B. gods   C. buffoons

6. Miranda and Caliban have this in common: _____
   A. they've been taught by Prospero to worship divine providence
   B. they have to listen to Prospero's lectures on chastity
   C. they have little experience of human beings other than Prospero

7. At the beginning of Act IV, Prospero lectures _____
   Ferdinand on the importance of
   A. chastity   B. patience
   C. penitence

8. The spirits' masque in Act IV ends because _____

   A. Prospero starts up in anger

   B. Ariel has to fetch Caliban, Stephano, and Trinculo

   C. Ferdinand talks and breaks the spell

9. The "three men of sin" are   _____
   A. Antonio, Sebastian, and Alonso
   B. Caliban, Stephano, and Trinculo
   C. Antonio, Sebastian, and Caliban

10. Prospero's farewell to his art has been   _____
compared to
   A. Queen Elizabeth's farewell to her reign
   B. Shakespeare's farewell to poetry
   C. Miranda's farewell to the island

11. Examine the play from a Christian point of view.

12. Discuss the pairing of characters. How does this technique help Shakespeare convey his themes?

13. Explain Prospero's fall from power in Milan. What lessons does he need to learn in order to become a good ruler?

14. Prospero calls Caliban "a born devil, on whose nature/Nurture can never stick." Discuss the themes of nature and nurture in *The Tempest*.

15. Consider Ferdinand and Miranda both as representatives of the play's themes and as characters. State your opinion as to their credibility.

ANSWERS

Test 1

1. A   2. A   3. B   4. A   5. C   6. B
7. C   8. C   9. B   10. C

11. Because this question asks you to defend an opinion, you'll have to decide for yourself what you think of Prospero. You can find evidence either to defend him or condemn him.

If you want to defend Prospero, you can point to his many good qualities. He's a loving father. He's wise and scholarly. He commands Ariel only until he accomplishes his plan; then he frees him. He forgives his enemies, including Antonio and Sebastian, who don't seem to deserve forgiveness. His past errors—trusting too much in Antonio and Caliban—have been on the side of kindness.

But Prospero isn't perfect; he's a harsh, angry man. He breaks up the lovely masque for Ferdinand and Miranda when his anger overcomes him. He may have a sense of justice concerning his own wrongs, but he doesn't seem to mind if his own behavior hurts innocent people. Thus, he horrifies Miranda with his cruelty to Ferdinand; he lets kindly old Gonzalo weep while he punishes Alonso. In addition, his earlier foolishness has caused suffering. In giving Caliban too much freedom, he allowed the monster to attempt to rape Miranda. In giving Antonio too much freedom, he lost his dukedom in Milan. This resulted in dire consequences for the city in the form of the annual tribute that Milan, under Antonio, must pay Naples.

12. This theme develops mainly in connection with Miranda, Ferdinand, and Caliban. Miranda associates beauty with moral goodness. Thus, in her "brave new world" speech in Act V, she assumes that because Alonso's party *looks* noble—"How beauteous mankind is!"—they must *be* noble: "How many *goodly* creatures are there here!" Shakespeare's audience really did associate goodness with beauty; after all, according to the Bible, God created humanity "in his own image." Miranda has two additional reasons to make this association. First, Ferdinand is extremely good-looking, a "thing divine," and she's in love with him. Second, her main experience of evil has been the ugly Caliban. Prospero notes that Caliban becomes even uglier as he grows more evil: "as with age his body uglier grows,/So his mind cankers." Caliban's mother, too, was evil and deformed: the "foul witch Sycorax" was "grown into a hoop" with "age and envy." But by including Antonio and Sebastian among the creatures whom Miranda calls "goodly," Shakespeare reminds you that reality is more complex than this simple symbolism.

13. The three plots in *The Tempest* are (1) Antonio's plot, with the aid of Alonso and Sebastian, to usurp the dukedom from Prospero, a dozen years before the beginning of the play; (2) Antonio and Sebastian's plot to kill Alonso and Gonzalo and make Sebastian King of Naples; (3) Caliban, Stephano, and Trinculo's plot to kill Prospero and make Stephano ruler of the island.

All three of these schemes aim to replace a rightful ruler with a wrongful one.

Antonio and Sebastian's plot against Alonso parallels the original plot against Prospero, and it serves two functions. First, because Shakespeare observed the classical unities and restricted the action of *The Tempest* to one day, he sacrificed certain dramatic possibilties. It's less exciting to have Prospero simply tell Miranda about the plot than it would have been to show it. But by introducing a new plot that's so similar to the original one, Shakespeare retains some of the drama without having to spread the action over twelve years. Second, although Prospero tells Miranda of Antonio's villainy, you also witness it; thus, it makes a much stronger impression upon you.

The Caliban-Stephano-Trinculo plot parodies the Antonio-Sebastian plot as well as the original plot. Its function is mainly comic, though it relates thematically to the rest of the play because it again shows characters attempting to rise above their proper place in society.

14. Although Ariel and Caliban are both magical beings of Prospero's island, they are opposites. Ariel is light, airy, intelligent; Caliban is heavy, earthbound, stupid. When Prospero summons Ariel, the spirit arrives as quickly as thought; when he calls Caliban, the monster complains and delays as long as he can.

The beings are also opposed in their sense of morality. Caliban is amoral. He shows no remorse about his attempted rape of Miranda. When he plots with Stephano and Trinculo to kill Prospero and seize the island, he gives no thought to the morality of his actions. Ariel, in contrast, is an extremely moral character. His speech to the "three men of sin" in Act III is practically a sermon on the classic Christian message of the necessity of repentance. Moreover, Ariel has suffered for his goodness: Caliban's mother, the "foul witch Sycorax," imprisoned him in the cloven pine tree because he was "too delicate" to carry out her horrible commands.

Ariel and Caliban do resemble each other in their desire for freedom. But Ariel craves freedom because it's part of his nature to be free; although he serves Prospero loyally, having a master is alien to his makeup. Caliban, however, is by nature a slave; he only wants freedom because he's too lazy to work. When he acquires freedom, he misuses it. He needs a master to exercise the authority he can't muster over his own appetites.

15. Gonzalo is the embodiment of the good Christian: kind, cheerful, patient, faithful and—as you know from his actions when Prospero and Miranda were cast out to sea—charitable. Unlike Alonso, he never loses faith that Providence is watching over them or that they'll locate Ferdinand. Unlike Prospero, he never succumbs to anger, even when Antonio and Sebastian mock his attempts to cheer the King.

Gonzalo is also rather an old bumbler, however, and he talks too much. Even in his great speech on Providence, he continues for too long and says too much: his assertion that they all have acquired self-knowledge isn't true for Sebastian or Antonio, nor probably for Gonzalo either. But these shortcomings make Gonzalo a more believable character; perhaps they even make him more likable than he would be if he were always right.

Test 2
1. C   **2.** C   **3.** C   **4.** B   **5.** B   **6.** C
7. A   **8.** A   **9.** A   **10.** B

11. To answer this question you can point to several Christian themes, which fall into three general categories: providence and patience; forgiveness; repentance.

As Prospero tells Miranda, they were brought to the island by divine providence. A good Christian, like Gonzalo, has faith in this divine benevolence and patience with the circumstances of his life. A man of little faith, like Alonso, is impatient and pessimistic. You can also argue that Prospero embodies providence within the play, because he controls so much of the action and ultimately, despite his initial anger, forgives even his unrepentant enemies.

As to forgiveness, the main question throughout is whether Prospero will overcome his anger and forgive his enemies. Christians, of course, are expected to forgive. Revenge is not a Christian attribute. As Prospero observes, forgiveness is a nobler action than vengeance.

Closely related to the theme of forgiveness is the concept of repentance. Prospero tells Ariel that all he really wanted when he punished the "three men of sin" was to make them repent their wrongdoing. Ariel delivers this message in his harsh speech to the three after the banquet in Act III. In this action, Prospero again parallels the Christian God, who is ready to forgive any penitent wrongdoer. This parallel develops problems, however, when Prospero forgives Antonio and Sebastian, wrongdoers who don't repent.

12. Before answering this question, you might want to list the various pairs. Sometimes the pairing seems insignificant: Adrian and Francisco, Stephano and Trinculo, the master and the boatswain. Antonio and Sebastian are both evil, usurping brothers, but their similarities don't tell you much about their characters. You learn more when paired characters are contrasted. For example, Prospero's wisdom is more apparent when compared to Alonso's foolishness. At times, Alonso is also paired with Gonzalo, and Alonso's lack of faith is more evident in contrast with the kind old councilor's extreme patience and faith in providence. Ariel and Caliban are almost precise opposites, and you can argue that their opposition functions symbolically: Ariel represents spirit and intelligence, Caliban flesh and appetite. Ferdinand and Miranda are paired romantically, in a way that's traditional on stage as well as in life. The pairing gives the play an aura of symmetry and simplicity, and contributes to its magical, fairy-tale atmosphere.

13. Prospero tells the story of his downfall in Act I. You can argue that he lost his dukedom because his hunger for knowledge was too great. (In this aspect, he resembles Adam and Eve, who lost Eden after eating from the tree of knowledge because they wanted to become godlike.) He gave up ruling for study, foolishly turning over the reins of government to his brother Antonio and thus failing to observe degree, as Antonio wasn't the rightful ruler. He later erred similarly with Caliban, giving the creature more freedom and more education than were appropriate to his low degree.

Thus, Prospero must learn two important lessons. The first is a lesson in self-control: he must keep his hunger for knowledge in check so that he can properly attend to his duties as ruler. Secondly, he must use his authority to see that others don't exceed their proper degree; he must keep his subjects in their places.

14. To answer this question, you should focus on Caliban and Miranda. The theme of "nurture" refers to education; that of "nature" describes a person's general makeup. Miranda has a high nature—a noble temperament, a sense of morality, and ample self-control. She benefits from her education; Prospero's teachings make her a better person, and she becomes a fine young woman. Caliban, however, has a low nature that can't be educated. He has so little self-control that he tries to rape Miranda, and he so lacks any moral sense that instead of regretting his crime, he cries, "Would't had been done!"

Caliban, however, does exit on a positive note. His final speech—"I'll be wise hereafter,/And seek for grace"—suggests that even if he has the nature of a born slave, he may have learned, at least temporarily, to accept his low degree. In this he contrasts with the unrepentant Antonio and Sebastian, who can't excuse their villainy by claiming low natures.

15. Ferdinand and Miranda embody the theme of reconciliation. Through their love, their fathers—Alonso and Prospero—find a way to end their hostility.

Both Ferdinand and Miranda are contrasted with the low-natured Caliban. While Caliban is governed by his appetites, Ferdinand is a model of self-control. He has the discipline and the stamina to accomplish the burdensome tasks that Prospero assigns him. As he explains at the beginning of Act IV, he respects the value of chastity—unlike Caliban, the would-be rapist.

Miranda benefits from the education Prospero has given her; on the other hand, Caliban has only learned to curse. In addition, Miranda has acquired the advantages of education without the accompanying corruption of civilization. When she declares her love to Ferdinand in Act III, she's straightforward because she hasn't learned coyness or deception. Shakespeare's audience would certainly have regarded this innocence as a virtue.

You'll have to examine Ferdinand and Miranda's scenes closely to decide whether you think their characters are believable or too good to be true. They have all the virtues of high nature and fine education, and they may remind you of a fairy-tale prince and princess. Shakespeare has, however, included details that make them appear more human. For example, Miranda disobeys her father when she tells Ferdinand her name. Later, she demonstrates her naïveté by including Antonio and Sebastian among the "goodly creatures" she praises. Ferdinand has some human attributes also. He's impulsive enough to draw his sword against Prospero. At the beginning of Act IV, after he's exchanged some very admirable sentiments with Prospero on the subject of chastity, his future father-in-law has to reprimand him for embracing Miranda a little too warmly. You must decide whether or not these details make Ferdinand and Miranda come alive as real people.

Term Paper Ideas and other Topics for Writing

Themes

1. Discuss the Christian themes in the play.

2. Discuss the theme of education in *The Tempest*, especially as it relates to Miranda and Caliban.

3. Examine the theme of chastity in the play.

4. Consider the ways in which *The Tempest* reflects Shakespeare's views on the social hierarchy.

5. Examine the theme of repentance in the play. Explain why Prospero forgives Antonio and Sebastian even though they don't repent.

Characters

1. Do you think Prospero decides to forgive his enemies during his conversation with Ariel early in Act V, or before that? Support your opinion by citing evidence from the play.

2. Discuss Prospero's relationship with Ariel and what it tells you about the way each character regards authority and freedom.

3. Consider the villains of the play: Antonio, Sebastian, Alonso, Stephano, Trinculo, and Caliban. Which of them do you think should be judged most harshly? least harshly? What evidence do you have for your opinion?

4. Contrast Alonso with Prospero and Gonzalo.

5. The Victorian poet Robert Browning wrote a dramatic

monologue called "Caliban upon Setebos" in which Caliban reflects upon his mother's god. Compare Browning's Caliban to Shakespeare's. How are they alike? How do they differ?

Shakespeare's Method

1. The characters in *The Tempest* speak in different styles: coarse or elevated, natural or artificial, long-winded or terse, prose or poetry, and so forth. What do you learn about each character from the style in which he or she speaks?

2. Examine the various planes of reality in the play. Which elements give it a fairy-tale atmosphere? Which relate it to the real world?

3. In *The Tempest*, Shakespeare simplifies his approach to psychology as compared with his earlier plays. Describe this simpler method and the effects he achieves with it.

4. What does Shakespeare achieve, or fail to achieve, by observing the classical unities in *The Tempest*? (Be sure to define the classical unities.)

5. Discuss the comic subplot of Caliban, Stephano, and Trinculo, explaining how it parallels the main plot and how these parallels function.

The Masque

1. How does the masque in Act IV relate to the themes of the rest of the play?

2. Compare the masque with other masques of Shakespeare's time, such as those by Ben Jonson.

3. Consider the masque-like elements that appear throughout *The Tempest*, in addition to the actual masque in Act IV. To do this, you'll want to read further about Renaissance masques.

Shakespeare's Other Works and *The Tempest*

1. Compare the verse style of *The Tempest* with the verse style of earlier plays by Shakespeare.

2. Compare *The Tempest* to one or more of Shakespeare's other romances: *Pericles*, *Cymbeline*, and *The Winter's Tale*.

3. Compare and contrast Ariel and the mischievous sprite Puck of *A Midsummer Night's Dream*.

4. Consider Trinculo in relation to some of Shakespeare's other clowns, such as Touchstone in *As You Like It*, Feste in *Twelfth Night*, the gravediggers in *Hamlet*, or the Fool in *King Lear*.

Other Topics

1. Examine the songs in the play. How do they function in the overall structure? How do they relate to the plot?

2. Analyze, line by line, one of the following speeches: Caliban on the island's music (III, ii, 140–148); Ariel to the "three men of sin" (III, iii, 53–82); Prospero after the masque (IV, i, 146–163); Prospero's farewell to his art (V, i, 33–57); Gonzalo on providence (V, i, 200–213).

3. Discuss the role of magic in *The Tempest*.

Further Reading
CRITICAL WORKS

Auden, W. H. "The Sea and the Mirror" (1944), in *Collected Longer Poems*. New York: Random House, 1969. A poetic commentary on *The Tempest*.

Coleridge, Samuel Taylor. *Coleridge on Shakespeare: The Text of the Lectures of 1811–12*, ed. R. A. Foakes. Charlottesville: University Press of Virginia, 1971. Lecture 9 focuses on *The Tempest*.

Eastman, A. M., and G. B. Harrison, eds. *Shakespeare's Critics, from Jonson to Auden: A Medley of Judgments*. Ann Arbor: University of Michigan Press, 1964.

Felperin, Howard. *Shakespearean Romance.* Princeton: Princeton University Press, 1972. *The Tempest* in the context of the late plays.

Kermode, Frank, ed. *The Tempest*. The Arden Edition of the Works of William Shakespeare. Sixth Edition. New York: Random House, 1964. An excellent edition of the play, with a helpful introduction and thorough notes.

Knight, G. Wilson. *The Crown of Life*. London: Methuen, 1948.

―――. *The Shakespearian Tempest*. Third edition. London: Methuen, 1953. (Originally published in 1932.) Both this and the later, more thorough *Crown of Life* view *The Tempest* as the culmination and summation of Shakespeare's great themes.

Nagler, Alois M. *Shakespeare's Stage*. Trans. Ralph Manheim. New Haven: Yale University Press, 1958. Shakespeare's performance space considered.

Schoenbaum, S. *William Shakespeare: A Compact Documentary Life*. New York: Oxford University Press, 1977.

Smith, Hallett, ed. *Twentieth Century Interpretations of The Tempest*. Englewood Cliffs, N.J.: Prentice-Hall, 1969. A collection of critical essays with a variety of approaches.

Tillyard, E. M. W. *The Elizabethan World Picture*. New York: Macmillan, 1944. How Shakespeare's audience viewed their universe.

―――. *Shakespeare's Last Plays*. London: Chatto and

Windus, 1938. Rebirth as part of the pattern of tragedy; planes of reality within the play.

Tobias, Richard C., and Paul G. Zolbrod, eds. *Shakespeare's Late Plays*. Athens, Ohio: Ohio University Press,
1985. Recent essays.

Traversi, Derek. *Shakespeare: The Last Phase*. New York:
Harcourt Brace, 1955.

AUTHOR'S WORKS

Shakespeare wrote 37 plays (38 if you include *The Two
Noble Kinsmen*) over a 20-year period, from about 1590
to 1610. It's difficult to determine the exact dates when
many were written, but scholars have made the following intelligent guesses about his plays and poems:

Plays

1588–93	*The Comedy of Errors*
1588–94	*Love's Labor's Lost*
1590–91	*2 Henry VI*
1590–91	*3 Henry VI*
1591–92	*1 Henry VI*
1592–93	*Richard III*
1592–94	*Titus Andronicus*
1593–94	*The Taming of the Shrew*
1593–95	*The Two Gentlemen of Verona*
1595	*Richard II*
1594–96	*A Midsummer Night's Dream*
1596–97	*King John*
1596–97	*The Merchant of Venice*
1597	*1 Henry IV*
1597–98	*2 Henry IV*
1598–1600	*Much Ado About Nothing*
1598–99	*Henry V*
1599	*Julius Caesar*

1599–1600	*As You Like It*
1599–1600	*Twelfth Night*
1600–01	*Hamlet*
1597–1601	*The Merry Wives of Windsor*
1601–02	*Troilus and Cressida*
1602–04	*All's Well That Ends Well*
1603–04	*Othello*
1604	*Measure for Measure*
1605–06	*King Lear*
1605–06	*Macbeth*
1606–07	*Antony and Cleopatra*
1605–08	*Timon of Athens*
1607–09	*Coriolanus*
1608–09	*Pericles*
1609–10	*Cymbeline*
1610–11	*The Winter's Tale*
1611–12	*The Tempest*
1612–13	*Henry VIII*

Poems

1592	*Venus and Adonis*
1593–94	*The Rape of Lucrece*
1593–1600	*Sonnets*
1600–01	*The Phoenix and the Turtle*

The Critics

On Caliban

The character of Caliban is wonderfully conceived: he is a sort of creature of the earth, partaking of the qualities of the brute, and distinguished from them in two ways: 1. By having mere understanding without moral reason; 2. By not having the instincts which belong to mere animals.—Still Caliban is a noble being: a man in the sense of the imagination, all the images he utters are drawn from nature, and are all highly poetical; they fit in with the images of Ariel: Caliban gives you images from the Earth—Ariel images from the air. Caliban talks of the difficulty of finding fresh water, the situation of Morasses, and other circumstances which the brute instinct not possessing reason could comprehend. No mean image is brought forward, and no mean passion, but animal passions, and the sense of repugnance at being commanded.

> —Samuel Taylor Coleridge, from a
> lecture on Shakespeare, 1811

On Prospero

Prospero is the central figure of *The Tempest*; and it has often been wildly asserted that he is a portrait of the author—an embodiment of that spirit of wise benevolence which is supposed to have thrown a halo over Shakespeare's later life. But, on closer inspection, the portrait seems to be as imaginary as the original. To an irreverent eye, the ex-Duke of Milan would perhaps appear as an unpleasantly crusty personage, in whom a twelve years' monopoly of the conversation had developed an inordinate propensity for talking. These may have been the sentiments of Ariel, safe at the Bermoothes; but to state them is to risk at least ten years in the knotty entrails of an oak, and it is sufficient to point out, that if Prospero is wise, he is also self-opinionated and sour, that his gravity is often another name for pedantic severity, and that there is no character in the play to whom, during some part of it, he is not studiously disagreeable.

> —Lytton Strachey, "Shakespeare's
> Final Period," 1922; reprinted in
> *Twentieth Century Interpretations
> of "The Tempest,"* ed. Hallett
> Smith, 1969

On the Scarcity of Metaphor

... *The Tempest* will be found peculiarly poor in metaphor. There is the less need for it in that the play is itself metaphor. Shakespeare's favourite imagery of storm and wreck cannot powerfully recur as descriptive comparison since the whole play, as its title announces, revolves round that very conception. ... Usually Shakespeare's tricks of pictorial suggestion can be felt as playing over and interpreting a story, though too rigid a distinction is dangerous; here there is no interpretation; the story is, or is supposed to be, self-explanatory; the creative act is single. It might be called Shakespeare's "purest work of art"; though whether purity, in art or in moral doctrine, itself so severe in *The Tempest*, is the whole of wisdom remains arguable.

> —G. Wilson Knight, *The Crown of Life*, 1947

On Antonio

"Good wombs," says Miranda, "have borne bad sons"—in the realm of the better nature there are "unnatural" men. ... Obviously among the better natures there were those upon whom some encounter or accident might beget an evil nature; that from the seed could grow degenerate plants. Many reasons were alleged to explain this, some astrological, some theological; and ultimately noblemen do ill because, being sons of Adam, they are free to choose. ... Caliban has no choice but to be vile; but in Antonio there was surely a predisposition to virtuous conduct; and it could not be easy to think of one who, in the eyes of Caliban, was a "brave spirit", as the betrayer of the fulness of his own more perfect nature, as a man so unnatural as to be impervious to the action of grace, a Macbeth of comedy. We see in Antonio the operation of sin in a world magically purified but still allowing freedom to the will; inhabitants of this world can abase themselves below those who live unaided at the level of nature. And it is as a comment upon his unnatural behaviour that we are offered a close structural parallel between Antonio's corrupt and Caliban's natural behaviour in the two plots against Alonso and Prospero.

> —Frank Kermode, Introduction to the Arden edition of *The Tempest*, 1954

On the Younger Generation

Not only do Ferdinand and Miranda sustain Prospero in representing a new order of things that has evolved out of destruction; they also vouch for its continuation. At the end of the play Alonso and Prospero are old and worn men. A younger and happier generation is needed to secure the new state to which Prospero has so painfully brought himself, his friends, and all his enemies save Caliban.

> —E.M.W. Tillyard, *Shakespeare's Last Plays*, 1958

On Gonzalo

The Renaissance voyagers [who wrote the Bermuda pamphlets], in their casting about for classical and Christian analogues to their experience, in their eagerness to see the miraculous at work and the special providence of God in all that happens, to see hope in disaster and lessons in trials, remind us more than a little of Gonzalo. From his comments on the breakdown of shipboard discipline during the opening storm to his wishful celebration of everyone's self-recovery near the end, Gonzalo tries, like the Renaissance voyagers behind him, to see a providential design in the experience of the play, to moralize that experience into what the Renaissance would call an "allegory." In doing so, although he does not "mistake the truth totally," as Antonio claims, he does have to bend reality ever so slightly to the desires of his mind and to that extent falsify it; not quite everyone, for example, has found himself by the end of the play as Gonzalo would like to think. His allusions to Carthage and "widow Dido" do distort Virgil in the strenuous effort to hammer out the parallel, and are representative of his efforts at perception throughout. One such effort is his benevolent vision of an island utopia [Act II, Scene I, lines 152–173].

—Howard Felperin, *Shakespearean Romance*, 1972